CW01494840

A Woman's Work

What Comes Next Book Two

Katharine E. Smith

HEDDON PUBLISHING

Paperback ISBN 978-1-917824-10-1
Ebook ISBN 978-1-917824-11-8

Cover design by Catherine Clarke Design

www.heddonpublishing.com
www.facebook.com/heddonpublishing

Katharine E. Smith is an independent author of contemporary and literary fiction, including the bestselling Coming Back to Cornwall series.

A Woman's Work is the second full-length book of the What Comes Next series, which is preceded by *First Christmas*, a novella set at the beautiful Soulton Long Barrow, and *Falling Out of Stride*.

A Philosophy graduate, Katharine initially worked in the IT and charity sectors. She turned to freelance editing in 2009, which led to her setting up Heddon Publishing, working with independent authors across the globe.

Katharine lives in Shropshire, UK, with her husband, their two children, and two excitable dogs.

You can find details of her books on her website:

www.katharineesmith.com

Information about her work with other authors can be found here:

www.heddonpublishing.com

and

www.heddonbooks.com

For Leanne and Trish xxx

Dreaming

Annie is moving restlessly in her sleep, limbs tangled in her sheets and mind tangled in her dream. As is often the case these days, her dream involves me – and food.

"Olive?" I ask my dream daughter, passing a small bowl of them across the table. She and I are sitting in the shade of a pergola, on an Italian hillside. Tuscany, I think. The hills are lined with vineyards and the day is almost unbearably hot. Even in the shade, Annie is sweating. She swats at a fly which buzzes around her head.

I'm impressed by the level of detail within her dream, but it's not just the fly that's irritating her.

"I already said no," she says, pushing the bowl away.

Dream-me smiles benignly at her but Annie feels an uncomfortable guilt at how she's treated me, and at feeling annoyed at me.

She wakes suddenly, with a gasp, and stares at her bedside clock.

2.34am.

It's a long time till morning.

She moves onto her side and stares at the empty space formerly occupied by Alex. She still has not got used to having a whole bed to herself, and she somehow can't bring herself to stray onto 'his side'.

An uncomfortable awareness creeps through Annie as her dream sits just out of reach but a residual guilt remains, directed towards me. She can't quite think why she is feeling that way but she surprises herself with a sob at the thought, yet again, that I am gone.

"Mum," she whispers into the darkness. Then as if at the sound of her voice, within her she feels that now familiar rummaging, jostling for space, and she smiles. Lays her hand on her stomach.

I smile too. Annie is not alone.

But all of a sudden, she is upright. Dashing for the bathroom. A wave of nausea has her dry -heaving over the toilet and I feel guilty now, that the dream version of me was offering her food when I know how sick she's been feeling. This pregnancy is not being easy on her.

So many things make her feel sick. A taste. A smell. A texture. Even the sound of certain songs which have accompanied her 'morning sickness' – which, I might say, is by no means confined to the mornings.

Poor Annie. She is not one to be sick. She's had three days off ill her entire working life and even when she was at school she would fight to go in when her brother or sister would have been pushing for the day off at the merest hint of a tickle in their throats. Even when I was ill, and when I died, she was loath to take time off work. Her manager Jeff insisted on it but Annie wasn't off for long.

It keeps her going, you see, her work. It's her leveller. Without it, she is lost. Right now she is thinking that when she has the baby she will only take a minimal amount of maternity leave. She is looking for a childminder who takes young babies, but Annie's exacting standards are making this search difficult. Alex of course wants his share of time with their child and he's talking about cutting his working hours – which Annie has no problem with. When he mentions his mum and dad taking the baby for a day a week, however, she feels a bit different.

It's not that Annie doesn't like Alex's parents. Although it's not exactly that she likes them either. But she knows without a doubt that Celia and James will not be like her, they already have very set ideas, and they do not match hers. If Annie is paying a childminder, she can specify how her baby should be cared for. Which nappies should be used (disposable, she's thinking right now); which milk formula (she's damned if she's going to be locking herself in a room at work rigged up to a breast pump like a cow in a dairy). When it comes to time to wean the baby (yes, Annie of course is already thinking this far ahead), she wants baby-led weaning. Healthy foods. Alex, she knows, even though they are no longer together, will do what she wants, how she wants it. His parents, she thinks, will not. She can just imagine Celia rolling her eyes and tutting at these modern notions of parenting. And Annie knows exactly what Celia thinks of her.

That she's too wrapped up in work, and that's why her marriage to Alex has failed. Of course, Alex's mum knows nothing of Alex kissing Annie's sister. Annie, valiantly, is willing to allow her erstwhile in-laws to think that the breakdown of the marriage is all down to her. And really, she thinks, they are right. Yes, Alex kissed Kitty, which sounds absolutely awful, but Annie is honest to a fault, especially when it comes to her faults. She knows she has never been the wife Alex wanted. Never given him as much affection, attention or reassurance of her love as he craved, and deserved. No, in their relationship she had the traditional 'masculine' role. She was the one who never really looked ahead or gave their future enough thought. She didn't pay a lot of attention to Alex's feelings, and she could not be the tactile, affectionate wife that he wanted. But he loved her, and she did love him. They just were far from the perfect match.

"Are you still in love with me?" he had asked her, more than once. She had not known how to respond. What did being in love even mean?

The first time, she'd drawn him to her and kissed him, taken him to bed, though she hadn't really felt like it. But it had seemed to answer his question satisfactorily and afterwards they'd lain together, and it had felt good. His hot, heavy body next to hers. She'd let him put his arm round her, though really she would have preferred just to have rested side by side. In time he'd fallen asleep. Annie had waited till he was breathing deeply and then she had gently pushed herself up and away from him, and looked at his face. He looked young, and his mouth was curved into a half-smile. Annie had felt something for Alex then – a wave of warmth and affection. Was that what being in love meant? It was a puzzle to her. Softly, she had slid out of their bed and padded across to the bathroom, shutting the door behind her. She turned on the shower, letting the water turn hot to the point of almost scalding before she stepped into it, watching her reflection in the mirror become slowly obscured by clouds of steam.

1

I stay with my daughter now, while she wrestles with her wakefulness, and I remember those nights during my own pregnancies when, no matter how tired I was, I just could not shut down, neither my mind nor my body.

With Annie, my first, I had many a sleepless night. I would wake with a start, maybe as a result of the increasingly weird dreams I used to experience or perhaps one of her sharp elbows catching me unawares. I remember trying not to wake Graham, and sometimes getting up and going downstairs, warming some milk and settling down on the sofa with my drink and a book, trying to lose myself in the story and not let the anxiety of impending motherhood distract me.

With Kitty, it was not so bad. I had worked out a few things I'd had doubts over, like how would I know when the baby was hungry (she'd cry), or need her nappy changing (she'd cry), or when it was time for a nap (she'd cry). But this second time, having experienced such a depth of love for my first child, I was worried about whether I'd be able to feel the same for a second. Surely it wasn't possible to love anyone as much as I loved Annie. Did I have enough love to spare? Always scrupulously fair whenever I could be, I was worried in my second pregnancy that I might favour Annie over her younger sibling. What if I resented the new baby muscling in on the incredible closeness I had with my first child?

Again, fearful of waking Graham and now of waking Annie too, I would tiptoe down the stairs, into the kitchen, and warm some milk, but I was too tired to read. I would turn on the radio very quietly and I'd just sit, feet up and legs stretched along the cushions, my mug clutched between my hands, sometimes resting lightly on my rounded belly, and I'd sip my milk and feel myself nodding off but it seemed like it was almost guaranteed that as soon as I began to fall into any kind of sleep, Annie would wake up, and start crying. And Graham, of course, would not wake at the sound of our daughter. It would be up to me to pull my tired body back up those stairs, and into Annie's room, where I could lift her onto my lap and comfort her till she fell asleep in my arms and I didn't dare move for fear of waking her again. It felt preferable to just sit there with my eyes closed, the weight of my sleeping girl on my lap, and let my thoughts come and go. I would try to attain a kind of meditative, dreamlike state. I was so tired that I often succeeded.

In the mornings, Graham would come looking for me, and he'd touch me gently on the shoulder. If I was lucky, he'd hand me a cup of tea, take Annie off me and downstairs, and I could crawl into bed for a few minutes – sleep-deprived but grateful for a bit of space and peace and a hot cup of tea to set me up for the day.

I think by the time I was pregnant with Tom, I had it down to a fine art. Thankfully, Annie was sleeping through by then, and Kitty was just a dream baby when it came to night-times. Still I would wake, suddenly, but I'd be so tired that I would find the off switch in my mind and I'd close my eyes and it wouldn't be long before I was back to sleep. It was only when I was about seven months pregnant and this baby seemed to be the same size as both the others put together, if my belly was anything to go by, that I had any real problems. I was so uncomfortable I'd just nap when I could, which wasn't often given I had two other small children to look after, but sometimes my mum or Graham's would take them off my hands for me, and give me a break.

When I think of Annie now eschewing Alex's parents' offer of help, although I understand why, I think she is making a mistake. I hope that she changes her mind. I would give anything for it to be me there, helping her, but this is just the way it is. And Celia is not a bad person, though she may be a bit set in her ways, and although Annie has so many fixed ideas herself about how to raise her baby – and she has every right to, although she does need to remember this is Alex's baby too – I know now that those things don't really matter in the long run. Whether the baby learns to feed itself or is spoon-fed, is it really that important, just as long as it is fed? Does it matter in the long run, if it follows a rigid routine? I do realise this one is really imperative to Annie as it will help her manage her life; she needs that in order to keep her mind calm and ordered. But babies are not ordered. They are unpredictable and prone to being sick or having rashes, or high temperatures, which throw everything out of the window. If only I could be with Annie to help her through the less manageable times, when I think she might struggle most. I would love so much to be able to reassure her, if the baby isn't hitting the 'milestones' detailed in books and discussed in online forums. I would give almost anything to be able to assuage her doubts and tell her that everyone worries they're not doing it right. Everyone fears that they are not enough. These are the times Celia really could be worth her weight in gold, if Annie would just let her.

As with everything these days with my family, I can do little more than hope, and watch, and hope again.

"I can only imagine," Teresa says, wistfully, when I express these thoughts, back in the deep, dark peace of our long-barrow home. Her son Derek has never had what you might call a serious relationship, and shows no signs of changing this situation any time soon. "I'd love a grandchild," my friend continues. "I know Val would too. She'd make a wonderful grandmother."

I love the way Teresa talks about Val. The sheer love and admiration that she makes no attempt to hide. The two of them got together when Derek was a schoolboy; his father, Teresa's ex-husband, was hard-going, by the sound of things, but it had taken quite a while for Teresa to decide to leave. I find it hard to imagine now, her being cowed by a bully of a man, and his mum, who they lived with. The Teresa I know would not be browbeaten by anyone. But Teresa back then had not been allowed to work or have her own money – "His mum took care of the *housekeeping allowance*," Teresa has told me, stressing the words sarcastically – and her spirit and confidence had been suppressed for some time. She knew that Derek wasn't happy but he was at a good school, famous for its academic successes, and Teresa worried that taking him away would dash his chances. Only once she realised she could stand it no longer, and she'd hatched and then enacted an escape plan, did she see just how unhappy Derek had been. He stayed on at the school, where his dad had gone too, and he remained a boarder there, though he'd begged Teresa to let him be at home. But she knew she had to make some kind of concession to her ex, who had threatened to withdraw all financial support for Derek if she enrolled him in a state school…

"It was just bad luck, really, that Derek often succumbed to stomach bugs which meant he had to be home with me, rather than risk spreading the germs through the dorms," Teresa has told me with a grin. "I know he didn't get such good grades as he might have done but by God he was happier than he'd ever been. Once he realised I was on his side and I was listening, although I couldn't get him away from the place completely, he knew I was there for him, and he blossomed. Really, he did. It was like that book *Patrick*, by Quentin Blake, do you know it?" I shook my head. "Oh, it's wonderful. This man Patrick, when he plays his violin, it breathes life into things. Makes fish fly, and makes hot buttered toast grow on trees. And there are two children in it, Kath and Mick I think they're called, and when Patrick plays his violin they go from kind of dirty, crumpled children to rosy-cheeked, with bright clothes, and ribbons in Kath's hair and…" Teresa smiled, seeing she was losing me. "I felt like I was Patrick," she clarified. "There was colour in Derek's cheeks. And a smile on his face. And he lost this kind of gaunt look he'd had." She shook her head, remembering. "I can't believe I put him through it for so long."

"You didn't put him through anything," I remind her. "They did. Your ex-husband, and his mum."

"Yes, but I let them."

"It's not as simple as that. You know it's not," I had said, and she'd smiled, acknowledging the sad truth.

11

"He might surprise you yet," I say now.

"He might. I mean… I know now, he's not gay. I always had my suspicions…"

Teresa has already told me this, more than once. While Derek was growing up she'd been waiting for him to come out. She'd even prepared what she was going to say to him, how she was proud of him and it mattered not a jot to her. But since she died and she's had the same level of insight into her family as I have into mine, she's realised he likes women, and has the occasional dalliance here and there, but he's not really driven to form a relationship.

"It's alright for men, isn't it?" Teresa slides easily into one of her favourite topics of conversation. "I mean, Derek's in his late thirties now. If he was a woman we'd be hearing the ticking of the biological clock, wouldn't we? Tick tock, better hurry up and have a baby. God forbid you haven't found a man by that age! But Derek, well he could meet somebody in ten years' time and become a father without a second thought. I hope he's quicker than that though, if he's going to do it. He could do with Val being young enough still to have the energy to help out."

"If she's allowed to," I say, thinking of Teresa's hypothetical grandchild's hypothetical mum and Annie's feelings regarding Celia. "She might not want an interfering in-law."

"Val wouldn't interfere!" Teresa wastes no time jumping to her beloved's defence.

"No, I don't think for a minute that she would," I reassure her. "It's just how it goes sometimes."

"Sorry!" she says. "I know what you mean. Anyway, this is ridiculous. It's Annie having a baby, not Derek. It's so exciting! But it must be bittersweet."

It is. That's the word for it. Bittersweet. I'm so pleased for Annie. It won't be 'the making of her' but it will be good for her, becoming a mum. And right now, while she – because I already know that this baby will be a she – is not yet out in the world, I am as close to her as I can be. I never knew how thin the veil was between the worlds but, while this baby is already a physical being, and very much alive inside Annie, her spirit is close to mine. I can feel her, communicate with her. Give her a tiny little nudge, like when she woke her mum from that dream. I can wrap this little being in all the love I would have shown her in the physical world. I would have loved to be there, to know what it is like to hold her warm, solid body, even to hear her cry. The reassuring sound of life.

But I can never have that, and my granddaughter will never wave excitedly, spotting me in the audience at school plays, or sit in my lap while I read a bedtime story. I will just be a name, and a face in so many pictures that Annie and Kitty and Tom and Graham will show in a bid to keep me alive, and convey to my grandchild who I was. But right now Annie's baby can feel my presence. She knows I'm here. It's a magical thing indeed.

2

At home... my old home... the family home, let's call it that, Graham has just woken up. Mavis, beautiful spaniel, woke briefly too but decided it was far too early so she is snoozing on beside him, keeping my side of the bed warm and full.

Graham is another one who cannot and will not get used to having a whole double bed to himself. I completely understand. While Annie has wished many times that she did not have to share with Alex, it's been a long time since Graham felt like that about me. I don't like to belittle his feelings when he was having his affair but back then I am sure he would have liked 'her' to be there instead of me.

I was mis-shapen, battered and bruised after three pregnancies and, unbeknown to us at the time, the illness that was taking hold of my body. I was distracted and probably a little bit depressed, and certainly quite a bit stressed, with work and fretting about my capabilities as a mother. Torn between my children and my career. Knowing that my relationship with Graham was changing – had changed – and not sure how to put it right or whether I even wanted to.

And of course, the ultimate cliché – while I was trying to come to terms with these life-changing dynamics, Graham felt like the spotlight of my attention had moved away from him. He was right. It had to. But he'd enjoyed feeling so vitally important to me; those early years when we were together; our intense love and attraction to each other. I'd have done anything for him, and he knew it. He was my world.

But I grew a little bit older, and a little bit wiser, and my world grew considerably bigger. I just didn't have the energy to put into making everybody happy. I heard friends talk about 'making time for' their husbands and how they'd have sex with them because they believed that was what men needed and deserved, or at the very least what they should do to keep them happy. I wasn't sure about that. To me, sex has always been something you should do only if you want to. Not to appease your partner or to make somebody else feel good at your own expense. And naturally, in my exhausted state, I didn't often want to have sex with Graham, or anybody else. If ever we had some spare moments, I just wanted to stop everything. Collapse on the sofa or on the bed. Yes, I'd love to have an early night, thanks. But it wasn't code for anything. I just wanted to sleep.

Of course, now I know my illness was also affecting how I felt, but we were at first unaware that there was anything wrong and I put my fatigue down to the wear and tear of having three children under five. I was having to learn at pace and I was also learning that Graham wasn't particularly interested in the ins and outs of parenting. Yes, he loved the children and yes, he was lovely with them. He enjoyed reading to them and playing with them, but when it came to the finer details, well his mind just seemed to be elsewhere. Probably in his secretary's ample bosom. Sorry, I couldn't help myself. That's a seaside postcard image and not even true. I'm sure she was a perfectly nice woman and no doubt heartbroken when he ended things between them.

And back to the present anyway. Now, he misses me keenly; heartbreakingly so. I became the centre of his world once he realised he could have lost me to that first illness. Now he's lost me to another, and he is lost in his life.

He gazes forlornly at the ceiling and wonders what it's all about. What's the point, of anything? He still loves our children but something about it feels a bit blurry and distant. They're adults now, of course, and need him less than they used to.

But they do still need you, I urge him, but he isn't listening.

In the soft light that falls through the gap in the curtains, dust motes swirl, glittering and glimmering in a bid to cheer him up. I blow softly, making them dance. Graham sees this and subconsciously takes it in.

"Dad?" Graham jumps at the knock on the door and Mavis twitches, but she's too old to leap up with glee as she once would have.

"Kitty?" my husband asks, tentatively.

"Do you want a cup of tea?"

Our middle child, our younger daughter, pushes the bedroom open tentatively and Graham pulls himself up to sitting. Mavis grumbles and shuffles around, nestling into the duvet.

"That… that would be lovely." Graham coughs to clear his throat. "But I should be making you one!"

"Oh don't worry about that," says Kitty. "I'm already up and dressed." She steps through the door to illustrate her point.

"So you are. OK then, Kit, I wouldn't say no."

"I'll be right back."

She's as good as her word and soon returns with a mug for Graham, which he accepts gratefully.

"Me and Tom… *Tom and I*," she grins at Graham before he can correct her, "were thinking of going to the barrow. He's meeting Cecily up there and I want to go and visit before I head back. Do you want to join us? It's a beautiful day."

"Sure," says Graham. "That sounds like an excellent idea."

"Brilliant. We were planning to go in an hour or so, no rush."

"Lovely. I'll drink this then I'll get up and showered."

"Great." Kitty turns to go and this time Mavis deigns to accompany her. She's slow on the stairs now, and Kitty sees this. "Oh Maeve," she says, ruffling our old dog's head. "Is it painful?"

Mavis just looks at her through tired eyes.

"I can carry you…?" Kitty asks tentatively, moving her arms onto Mavis's sides, but Mavis emits a low growl.

"That's OK," Kitty says. "I get it."

Mavis hobbles along, her joints sore and tired, but she follows Kitty through to the kitchen and then out into the garden. Kitty's brought her mug with her and she sits in the arbour while Mavis wanders around and takes in the smells of the new day.

"Alright sis? Where's my brew?" Tom emerges into the sunshine.

"Get your own!" laughs Kitty. "Actually, I did make you one, it's next to the kettle. I thought you'd see it."

"I hear Dad got his brought to him."

"Well yes, but he deserves it."

"Hmm."

It's good to see the old ease has returned to Kitty and Tom's relationship, after their falling out a couple of months ago. It didn't amount to anything much; it didn't have a chance to, with Tom having his accident and ending up in hospital, but I've always felt a little bit uneasy when all is not well between any of my children. I loved those golden days of their childhood when they would all play nicely together. I remember them squealing and laughing as they took it in turns to dash under the sprinkler. Why does it feel like all their childhood summers were like that, every day, when I know they were not? For one thing there is no chance that it was sunny and dry without fail, but those are the times that shine out and eclipse the long, tiresome indoor days when plasticine and Play Doh and paints and crayons would cover the dining room table and each activity would seem to only fill about fifteen minutes, and the grey sky and rain would make it so dark we'd need to have the lights on. Even those days held value though, and I'd love to see my children's little heads bent over their projects, and sometimes I'd find time to just stand and have a quiet cup of tea while I watched them. Annie could be quite teacherly and offer advice and, occasionally, praise to her younger siblings. They would glow in the light of her approval.

Tom returns to the garden with his cup of tea. He sits by his sister.

"Do you think Dad's OK?"

"Er – yeah, I think so. He seemed a bit spaced out when I went in, but I guess he'd just woken up."

"It'll be good when Annie has her baby, give him something new to think about."

"I hope so."

"He'll love it! He can buy it *My First Engineering Book*."

"That's not my calculator, its functions are too basic," Kitty laughs.

"We're going to have to make sure that kid gets some creative input," Tom says.

"Yes! I'm sure Alex might help to balance things out too," adds Kitty.

"He's going to have to fight hard to get any real involvement, knowing Annie. When it comes to decisions about, I don't know…"

"Education? Diet? Exercise? After-school clubs? What colour socks it's allowed to wear…?"

They laugh, not unkindly, but it makes me feel a little bit defensive towards Annie. Knowing they are laughing about her behind her back. But it's what siblings do, isn't it? Friends too. And spouses. Sometimes that's the way we try to rationalise the irrational side of those we love.

"We might have to help on that score too." And just Kitty saying this has me backing down. I know how much Annie's brother and sister care about her, and how they will help her to navigate when she's struggling.

"So are things OK with you all now?" Tom asks, eager to know more about what happened. He's got an inner gossip that he tries hard to deny but with mixed levels of success.

"Yeah, it's fine," Kitty says airily, and frustratingly. "How are things with Cecily?"

"They're pretty good," says Tom, and he can't help but smile.

"Good. Great, in fact! You know you two are made for each other, don't you?"

"Do you think?"

"God, yes, isn't it obvious?"

Tom is quiet for a moment. "And do you think," he asks quietly, "Mum would have approved?"

"Tom!" Kitty turns to her brother, tears glistening instantly in her eyes. "Of course she would. Mum really liked her, even though she didn't know her for long. And you know, it's obvious how much Cecily cares about you. And that she wants to make you happy. God, the way she looks at you… it would be sickening, if you weren't both so lovely."

Tom laughs.

"Mum would love to see you two together." Kitty puts her arm around her little brother's shoulder. "And you know she only ever wanted us to be happy. If Cecily makes you happy then you can be sure that she would approve."

Tom leans against his sister and they are both quiet for a moment, contemplating love, and life, and death. They feel a little whisper of breeze across their cheeks, which is the best I can do to try to let them know I'm there, and to let Kitty know she's right. I do very much approve of Cecily, and I do very much want my children to be happy.

3

While her sister and brother are getting ready to come out to visit 'me' at the barrow, Annie is also preparing to go out, but in her case she has the office in mind.

"On a Sunday?" Kitty had asked.

"Yes, on a Sunday," Annie replied with a genuine effort not to react defensively.

"Fair enough." Kitty knows her sister well enough not to argue, or cajole. "But if you change your mind you know where we are. And if you fancy coming for lunch, I'm cooking, before I head back to the flat." She wonders why she can't seem to call it 'home' when it comes to her family. Like it might offend them somehow, though she's been in that flat for years now. It is her home.

"I don't think I'll make it, sorry," Annie had replied with genuine remorse. "I wish you didn't live so far away."

"It's not a million miles," Kitty said softly. "You can be at my place in an hour and a half." She knows this is not really much comfort. "And Annie, you should. Come and visit before you get too pregnant."

"I don't think that's a thing," Annie said but she was smiling. "You're either pregnant or you're not."

"You scientific types!" Kitty had laughed. "You know what I mean though – before you don't feel able to drive long distances. Actually, maybe I should just come back here and see you…"

"I would love to come and see you," said Annie. "And I'll see if I can get back for lunch today then we can make a date."

"Brilliant, I'll make sure we set a place for you."

"Thank you, Kitty. I do appreciate it, you know."

"What?"

"You looking out for me. Looking after me."

"You'd do the same for me."

"I would."

Replaying this conversation, Annie glances in the mirror. She chooses not to notice the dark circles underneath her eyes, instead smoothing her eyebrows and picking up a nearby comb to make sure everything is as it should be before she leaves the house.

When she gets to the office, she lets herself in. She misses the cheery greeting Sam the security guard normally offers and she cringes as she remembers her recent conversation with him, where she was trying, so hard, to empathise. It does not come naturally to Annie, empathy. You may have already picked that up.

"So, Sam, I might come in this weekend," she had told him on her way out one Friday afternoon.

"No rest for the wicked, eh?" He'd grinned at her. He was one of the few people at work who seemed to treat her just like everybody else. Annie is well aware that she is deemed unapproachable by many of her colleagues – especially the younger ones and, most painfully, the younger female ones.

"No, something like that." She had tried a smile. "But I just wanted to let you know."

"OK, well thanks." She could see on his face that he wasn't quite sure what else to say.

"So... see you then I suppose," Annie had said, finding her toe-curling awkwardness closing in.

"Oh, I see what you mean. No, I won't be here. I don't work weekends."

"You don't?"

"No! I don't live here you know, Anne." (She is Anne at work – Annie would be far too familiar).

Sam had just laughed but she had felt a total idiot. For a long time she had felt sorry for Sam, imagining he must have to work all hours and having no idea what kind of a wage he might be earning but presumably not much of one. For Annie, this was a real kind of progress and an effort to be more socially aware but as it turned out she had probably been thinking very condescendingly. As though he must be hard up to be a security guard – presumably not educated very highly and not very well off.

"Of course you don't," she had said and, very unusually for Annie, she felt a blush begin to creep up her neck and crawl onto her cheeks. "Well, I suppose I'll see you Monday then."

"That you will," Sam had smiled and Annie had walked out, head held high, with no idea that Sam was still smiling as he watched her go. Then he shook his head. Ran after her.

"Anne!"

"Yes?" She'd turned.

"There's an alarm," he said. "You'll need to turn it off."

"Oh. Thanks. Of course."

"Hasn't Jeff told you?"

"No, I…"

She wasn't planning on telling Jeff she was coming in at the weekend. She knew he'd tell her not to. Tell her to put her feet up, go shopping for the baby. Since she'd told him she was pregnant she could swear he was already writing her off, placing her alongside his wife and so many other women who had given up their careers, put them 'on hold', when they became mothers.

But this is not what is going to happen to Annie, she is quite sure of that. So these weekend visits will be a secret. She will check through all her projects, dotting the Is and crossing the Ts, leaving nobody in any doubt that she, Annie Hebden (she kept her maiden name for her work and now she's glad that she did) is more than capable of her job, and is in fact essential to the running of this place.

And she knows now, as she should already have realised, that there is no need for a security guard at weekends because her colleagues – nice, normal people – don't work weekends unless they absolutely have to. But that doesn't bother my Annie. In fact, as she lets herself in and turns off the alarm, she hums to herself. She likes the stylish place where she works, with its spotless polished floors which gleam as she turns on the lights. And she likes it even more on a day like today, when there is not another soul around. She locks the door and then heads up the stairs to her office. She does not want to take the lift when there is nobody else here. What if it broke down and she got stuck? Besides, the stairs give her a bit of exercise.

Filling up her bottle at the water dispenser, she goes through to her office and settles in, checking the time. She could fit in a good three hours and still get back for Kitty's lunch. She really should be there, she thinks, especially as she hasn't been to the barrow with them this morning.

The clock on the wall provides the only noise, ticking off the time in an orderly fashion as Annie works. I watch her as she stares intently at her computer screen, opening various files and occasionally wheeling her chair back to her bookcase and plucking a hefty tome or a folder from it to cross-reference something. Don't ask me what she's doing;

I have no idea. For all my lengthy marriage to Graham, I had very little real idea of what he did for a living. I could tell you his job titles over the years but that was about as far as it went. Annie is the one who understands this side of him. Having said that, I don't suppose either of them really know half of what I did as a nurse. Some things are self-evident of course, to anyone who's ever had a medical appointment or a stay in hospital, but what you see as a patient is just the tip of a very large iceberg.

It's good to see Annie at work though, and the energy which emits from her. She is good at what she does, and she knows it. But she is also putting a bit too much pressure on herself. I know she is scared that this baby will change things, and the thing is, she's right. Life will never be the same again. If I could tell her that, I would. But I'd also say that just because becoming a mother will change things, it doesn't have to mean that they change for the worse. But even if I was there to tell her that, I know that until she experiences it for herself she won't understand. She can't know what it is to be a mum until she is one, and how the things that matter so much now, though they will still be important – and rightly so – will take on a different shade when this baby becomes a reality.

Motherhood is impossible to imagine. It is magical, daunting, exhausting… and at times incredibly boring. It turns your life upside-down, makes you question your place in the world, and your sense of worth. You have to put your own concerns in second place, but that doesn't make you a pushover, and it doesn't mean you are any less 'you'. If anything, it opens up new dimensions you never even knew about. And I can almost guarantee that when it comes to it, Annie's mind will be preoccupied with her baby. That may not sound very feminist but it's not about feminism. It's about love. And I went back to work when Annie was a few months old, and again after I had Kitty. It was not much the done thing then but I wanted to. I didn't want to fall behind, get out of practice. So I know in a way where Annie is coming from. I know she's scared of losing all she's worked for and, more than that, she is scared of losing herself. This, her work, is the version of the world that makes the most sense to her.

I'm glad that she's agreed to Kitty's offer of lunch. It means she won't be working all day, and I know she will unwind a little with her family around her. It also means she might eat a proper meal. Thankfully she's not feeling too sick today and in fact she's a little bit hungry. She heads to the kitchen in search of snacks, preferably ginger biscuits. As she pads across the floor – she has taken her shoes off, seeing as there's nobody else around – she starts at the sound of voices downstairs. Her heart begins to pound.

Did she not lock the door? She's sure she did. But – no that's definitely a man's voice, and not one she recognises. Annie stops stock-still, unsure what to do. Suddenly the exquisite peace of the empty office has developed a sinister undertone. But she's angry at the intruders – a) for interrupting her work and b) for potentially messing things up for her.

Oh my god, how much trouble will I be in if I've left the place unlocked? Baby brain, they'll blame it on. I'll be finished.

This is how my daughter's mind works; these are the concerns she reaches towards first. What this will do to her career. Then she feels that familiar shuffling within her and she realises with a thud, it's not her job that matters right now. It's this tiny being whose safety she has possibly mistakenly been trusted with. Shit. Her office door is open and her light is on. Her shoes are on the floor. It will be obvious that there's somebody here. What should she do? She could hide in the women's toilets. She almost laughs. As if any self-respecting burglar/attacker would be stopped in their tracks by the female sign on the door. And anyway, if she's hiding in the toilets how will she know when they've gone?

But then comes a second voice, and Annie could almost scream with relief. It's Jeff. She's sure it is. She hears his laugh. Yes it is. It's Jeff! As the voices come closer to the stairs, Annie tiptoes as fast as she can back to her office, for some reason concerned that Jeff and whoever she is with will see her without her shoes on.

"Hello?" she hears her manager call. Of course, he'll know there's somebody here. The lights are on, and the alarm was switched off. She slips her shoes on and smooths her hair.

"Hello?" Annie calls back, trying to sound surprised.

"Annie! What are you doing here?"

Jeff emerges at the top of the stairs, accompanied by a well-dressed man who looks a little bit younger than Annie.

"Oh hi," she says. "I was just going through a few bits on the Jennings proposal, you know. It's due this week and I just wanted to check everything's ready."

"Well that's very noble of you but shouldn't you be making the most of your weekend off?" Jeff's eyes are gazing at Annie's rounded tummy.

At least it's not my breasts, she thinks but still she wants to slap him, tell him to look her in the eye.

She sees the stranger's eyes also rest briefly on her pregnant belly, before he looks back up and smiles at her. He steps forward, hand outstretched. "Ryan Edwards," he says.

Annie takes his hand. "Annie Hebden."

"I guessed as much."

"Oh?"

"Yes, sorry," Jeff steps in, "I should have made the introductions. Annie, this is Ryan. He's currently with Glydon & Josephs but I hope he'll be joining us soon."

"Oh yes?" Annie asks.

"Yes," Jeff says, still staring rudely. "He'll be taking on your projects when you've left. To have your baby."

Ryan Edwards smiles benignly and Jeff finally looks up, while panic breaks out inside Annie. It appears that all her fears are about to come true.

4

"What a waste of time," Annie fumes, back in her car and on her way home. She had been so thrown by the news that she was about to be replaced, and so distracted by the sound of Jeff and Ryan talking and laughing as they roamed the place, drinking coffee and discussing the various projects that were on the go – many of them Annie's projects – that she just couldn't concentrate. And now, sitting in the driver's seat and heading along the country lanes back to our little town, it takes all her willpower not to slam her foot on the accelerator and let her car do the talking. She knows that would be stupid though, and potentially dangerous, for her and the baby and any other unwitting road user, and gradually, over the half-hour drive, she calms ever so slightly. Even so, she's not sure about going for lunch now. She doesn't feel like seeing anybody, even her brother and sister and dad – and knowing that Cecily will be there too, Annie is beginning to think she'll cry off. She really does like Cecily but she knows that being the pleasant, personable older sister she would like to present herself as will take a considerable effort today. She just doesn't think she has it in her.

No, Annie thinks, this afternoon she will do what everyone's been telling her to do – put her feet up. Have a nap.

Urgh, a nap, she thinks with disdain. *She's* not a baby, or an old lady for that matter. Still, the thought is increasingly attractive. And maybe she does need some downtime. To *reset*, she thinks sardonically. That's the type of word Kitty uses, and Cecily. They're all about taking time for yourself, being kind to yourself. That's all well and good, thinks Annie, but it's not going to get the work done. Deep down, though, she is envious of their relaxed attitude. She'd like to think like they do but she just can't.

And they're so bloody kind to other people too! Kitty has told her that she's invited that boss of hers to spend a night at her flat and offered to take care of the night watch at the kennels just so that Meg can have a break for once. Apparently the woman had been sleeping in her office during the winter as she couldn't afford to heat her own home as well as the place where the dogs lived.

"Well that's just stupid," Annie had said plainly. "She should be heating her home. Dogs have fur, don't they?"

"Yes, but they still get cold," Kitty had patiently explained to her sister. If it had been anyone else she'd have been up in arms and reading them the riot act about animal rights, but she knows Annie is just being typically pragmatic, rather than cruel.

"Do they? I suppose they must." Annie had shrugged. She does love Mavis, but generally when it comes to animals she can take them or leave them. She certainly can't fathom why Meg is sacrificing so much to look after these dogs which aren't even hers. She's even trying to find them new homes, and not for a profit either – and then taking new dogs in, though she is clearly struggling to keep afloat financially. It doesn't compute to Annie, but she is self-aware enough these days to realise that maybe the fault there lies with her, and her inability to see the world in the same way so many others seemed to. She wouldn't be offering the woman the use of her house for a night though, and certainly not at the expense of her own comfort. As far as Annie's concerned, Meg's made her bed and she should lie in it – or on the office floor, if that's what she prefers.

As she rounds the corner onto her street, she feels a tide of relief rising within her. It's been quite a morning, on top of a long, sleepless night. She can message Kitty to apologise, then make some lunch and maybe even take it into the lounge – eat in front of the TV instead of at the dining table like she always does, even now she's on her own. Maybe she'll find a film to watch, and hope it helps her unwind enough to get a little bit of sleep. She's happier now that she's made this decision. Her family will understand. She just doesn't need to see anyone else right now…

"Oh no," she says as she turns into her drive.

Alex.

"Hi," he says, opening her car door for her, never quite sure how to greet her these days.

"Hello Alex," she says resignedly.

"I was just about to go," he says. "I realised you were out."

No shit, Sherlock. Why didn't you just phone and ask? She's not too keen on his just turning up at her house like this but she finds it hard to say anything because legally it is still his house too. Is he checking up on her though? Surely he doesn't think she's got a new man…

"Been anywhere nice?" he asks, when no reply is forthcoming.

"Work."

"On a Sunday?" Alex unwittingly echoes Kitty's reaction.

"Looks like it."

"Shouldn't you be taking it easy?" he asks, though he knows how well this will be received.

"I'm OK, I'm going to have an easy afternoon." Annie often has to work very hard to remind herself that as well as this being Alex's house, this baby is his too and, though it's her doing all the growing, and carting around of it, he does have a right to care about its welfare.

"Oh. OK." He leaves it at that. "Have you had lunch?"

Annie thinks fast. She is fixed now on the idea of a quiet sandwich in front of the TV, the thought of it seeming delightfully slovenly. Maybe a bag of crisps on the side. She does not want Alex encroaching on this downtime she's allotted herself.

"No, I'm going to Dad's."

"I thought you were having an easy afternoon?"

Damn. She had not thought quickly enough. "Yes, I meant Kitty's cooking, and so I don't have to do anything. You know what she's like, and Tom, they'll look after me."

"Yes, they will." Alex looks sad now and I know he's missing the days he was included in these meals, without a second thought. He was part of the family, and now he's not. That stings. I can see that and I can understand it too.

"So…"

"So?"

"Why are you here?" Annie asks impatiently. She is desperate for a wee now she's home, and it's turning into quite a hot afternoon. She would like to get inside, and out of the sun, but she doesn't want to invite him in. She might never get rid of him.

"It can wait," says Alex.

"Oh?"

"Yeah, I'll give you a call during the week. Maybe we can have a catch up one night. Go out for tea or something?"

"I don't know, it's going to be a busy week. And I'm pretty tired."

"Well I'll phone you anyway," he says, annoyed now.

"Great."

"Great. Guess I'll be going then."

Alex gets in his car, slamming the door as hard as he dares, and he drives away. Annie pushes the key into the lock, leaving the front door swinging open in her desperate bid for the bathroom. Sighing with relief as she pulls down her trousers and underwear and sits on the toilet, she has a moment of panic that Alex might return and just wander in. Or a stranger, for that matter. But no, she is fine, and once she's finished she flushes the loo and washes her hands then walks out of the open front door into the garden, listening to a blackbird singing at the top of a conifer. It relaxes her, and she sits on the front doorstep in the shade, leaning back against the edge of the doorframe and letting the tiredness wash over her.

It's tough on Alex, she knows that. And she wouldn't want to be the one pushed out of their home. He's currently living at his parents', which can't be easy either.

At first Alex had tried to argue for staying in the marital home, taking one of the spare rooms: "Then I can look after you, while you're pregnant. It will make it easier when the baby comes too."

The thought had sent something like panic spinning

through Annie. Alex should have known that she wouldn't be able to deal with the blurred lines of such a living situation.

"I don't think so, Alex," was the kindest reply she could summon.

"But…"

"Alex," she had said sharply. "We are splitting up. We will be miserable if we're living in the same house. I will keep you informed about the pregnancy and I will let you know if there are any problems, and I will not push you out of the baby's life. You can come to all the appointments you like. But I cannot share a home with you."

"Bloody hell," Alex had gulped. "Why don't you say what you really think?"

Annie had just sighed, exasperated, trying very hard not to throw in his face the fact that he had kissed her sister.

And Alex, though he was not happy about it, had accepted the situation, and gone back to his mum and dad's.

"You need to get that house on the market, son," James had said. "She can't expect to have it all. She can't have her cake and eat it."

"She's not, Dad," said Alex, aware that he had never told his parents what happened with Kitty and so in their eyes the break-up was all down to Annie, who they had never been quite sure about if they were honest. "And I am not about to put her through the upheaval of moving house when she's going to be giving birth to our child soon."

"It *is* your child, Alex," Celia had said, with tears in her eyes. "Don't lose sight of that, will you? Don't let her push you out."

"She won't. Honestly. I know Annie. She may not be the most… feeling… of people, but she is fair to a fault." He put his arm around his mum's shoulder.

"She certainly doesn't deserve a good man like you," Celia said. "Now, what do you want for tea?"

At least his mum appreciated him, thought Alex, basking in the glow of her maternal love. "Can I have sausages and chips?"

"Of course you can. With beans?"

"Yes please, Mum."

"You're a good boy, Alex." Celia kissed him and bustled off to the kitchen, to look after her men. She wouldn't wish this marriage break-up on Alex – of course she wouldn't – but it was so nice to have him home again. Somewhere inside, a very small part of Alex wondered if this was part of the problem. That he was still his mum's 'good boy'. But he pushed the thought away and sat down next to his dad – who had gone back to reading the paper – picked up the TV remote and flicked through the channels, trying to find something to watch while he looked forward to his sausage, chips and beans.

5

I sit by Annie on her doorstep, feeling her heart rate and breathing adjust to the different thoughts and feelings currently trundling through her. Having been ambushed by Alex, then spending far longer than planned at the family lunch, she's only just now able to stop, and sit, and mull things over.

Ryan Edwards, she thinks, unnecessarily disparaging about his name. But she's assessed, correctly, the threat of him, to her work and her position there. It's not uncommon for a pregnant woman to be usurped by their 'maternity cover' and when that cover is male, well it's almost a given. A done deal.

She replays the sound of Ryan's and Jeff's male laughter as they strode around the office together, laying claim to it. This is Annie's perception. It's not one hundred per cent wrong but… *Oh Annie, my Annie.* It breaks my heart. She's so bloody proud and so bloody paranoid and so bloody aware that she does not see life as others do. That she doesn't slot neatly into the social scene or the 'water cooler conversations' if indeed they are a thing these days, the WhatsApp groups and the friendly female discussion about diets and clothes and what's on Netflix. And now, it seems, she is being pushed out of the higher echelons, the place she has carved for herself where satisfaction in her work can supersede that familiar 'odd one out' feeling and where she is listened to, and respected, woman or not.

The weakness, she thinks. The curse of women. Not periods, but a pregnancy, right when she's in her prime. When she's just pushing at that ceiling, wondering if she can crack it, or maybe even smash it. She pushes an angry tear away because it feels like she is being disloyal to her baby.

"It's not you I resent," she murmurs, placing her hand lightly on her belly. "It's the world." *And it's your dad*, she thinks, though it's not Alex's fault. And he doesn't even really like his job. Probably he'd jump at the chance to leave it altogether, and replace those long, tiresome days in the office with looking after his baby. But Annie does not think she can allow that.

Oh Annie, I think again. I ache for her.

Her thoughts turn now to the family lunch and as they do I feel her relax a little. I am so glad; so proud of my family, who might annoy and irritate each other but whose love is so strong, and unquestioned. Unconditional. In the time I've been gone, Kitty has kissed Annie's husband, and Tom and Kitty have fallen out to the point that Tom had stropped off and nearly killed himself – accidentally but that's not the point. Graham has been largely, but forgivably, absent, but despite all of this they are bound together. *With bonds that cannot be bro-oken,* I find myself thinking, remembering primary school assemblies.

Tom and Kitty had cooked, and Graham, Annie and Cecily had sat in the lounge, Graham drinking a beer, Cecily one of my sherries, and Annie carefully taking sips of a ginger ale, testing out her stomach. One thing that she's noticed today is that she hasn't felt as nauseous as usual. Mavis positioned herself next to Annie, as she has seemed to have done more and more since Annie became pregnant. She lies her head across the top of her right thigh and Annie finds she likes it. In fact, she likes the way that everyone seems more protective towards her at the moment. As she thinks of it now, tears glisten in her eyes. She is touched by how her family care.

Lunch was delicious too; Annie had piled her plate high with nut roast and Yorkshire puds, roast potatoes and veg.

"Definitely eating for two now, Annie!" Tom had laughed and Graham had shot him a look but Annie had actually laughed too.

"I think I'm making up for the last few weeks. I've not had much of an appetite. I've not been able to keep much down. Sorry, not the best topic for the dinner table."

"Ah that's rough," Cecily said. "Mum says she had the worst morning sickness with me. It's one of the reasons she didn't want another child."

"Plus she couldn't possibly have another child that would compare to you," Tom said, only half joking. Kitty made a mock-throwing-up gesture.

"Careful, Tom, I'm only just starting to feel better," Annie had said, and been gratified by the resulting laughter.

"It's true though." Cecily had grinned.

Graham had looked at them all at this point and thought, *I wish Ruth was here for this*, but for once he didn't say it. He's learning.

"So hopefully you're going to be on top form for London," said Kitty.

London. The trip is in two weeks' time, to coincide with Graham's and my wedding anniversary. Another first without me. They were thinking of going for my birthday but Tom couldn't book the time off work so the wedding anniversary it is.

"I hope so," Annie had said, wondering how to introduce the idea that she might not be able to go. How could she take a weekend away – a long weekend at that – knowing that her job was about to be pulled from under her? She had a deadline which was non-negotiable. In the autumn, this baby was going to turn up, giving her maybe another four months to make herself indispensable. To work her way into her projects, and her clients' hearts, to such an extent that to try and wedge Ryan into her place would be unthinkable.

But it was going to take some planning, and some effort. And every second – every weekend, certainly – was going to count. Assuming there would be no more unexpected interruptions as there had been this morning, Annie knew that weekends were invaluable. They presented her best chance of working as hard and as long as she needed to without somebody calling her, or one of her colleagues asking her advice on something.

"I'm really looking forward to it," Graham said, and Annie's heart sank. How could she let her dad down? "It will be good to be away from home on our … the… my–" he tried out the various options – "anniversary without your mum."

"Hopefully I'll be feeling much better for it," Annie said and I was proud of her, though I can feel now her heart pounding as she considers watching her career spiralling out of control and down the plughole. Of them all, Graham would understand if she didn't come, she reasons to herself, as they share so much in terms of work. She is close to something like panic as she pictures a future without a job. If they push her out when she's had the baby. It wouldn't be the first time that's happened to a new mum, she thinks. She's right. One of Kitty's old school friends, Jane, experienced her job being whipped away from her almost as soon as she had her first child. She was invited into the office when she was on maternity leave, ostensibly to introduce her baby to her work friends and colleagues. The evening before, Jane's manager – a woman, I might add; in fact, a mother herself – had messaged her to say perhaps it would be better not to bring the baby. This immediately set alarm bells ringing but, gamely, Jane went in anyway, to be greeted not by a welcome party but by her manager and a representative of HR, who whisked her away to an office and presented her with a new organisation chart, to compare to the current one. The only difference was that Jane's job was no longer there. She sat in shock, though not surprise, and barely took in what they were saying. There was no meeting with her other workmates; in fact, as she discovered later, they had no idea that she had been in. Over the following weeks, Jane was offered a few positions more junior to the one she'd been ousted from and after a while the stress began to get to her and she caved in, and decided to leave, reasoning that she had a baby to look after and her own health to take care of. She hasn't worked since; not paid work, at least. She is now a mum to two beautiful boys but her career and her National Insurance contributions have taken a battering – not to mention her confidence.

I am sure it will come as no surprise to you that shortly after Jane's departure from the company, a new position within her department was deemed necessary; it had a slightly different title to Jane's but a suspiciously similar job description.

Annie is privy to all of this and she's nervous, and

scared, though she wouldn't choose to use that word herself. It's not just the money, though as a single mum that is going to be important. It's the sense of self that comes with her work because, in Annie's mind, if she isn't working then, really, who is she?

6

It's been a long day and I am glad to return to the long barrow, which is surrounded by the sweet sound of birdsong, well into the evening. This is my favourite time of year and I'm so grateful that I can still enjoy it, though it's tinged with a sadness that I'm not able to sit with Graham in our garden, companionably reading and drinking tea or maybe sharing a bottle of wine, as we'd become accustomed to doing since the children grew up and suddenly we had our evenings back again.

Each year it felt like we had battled another winter together; though in honesty our winters are hardly Little House on the Prairie standard. But the mental aspect of winter, I do – I did – find difficult. The darkness was hard to bear. And the claustrophobia of being cooped up together too much.

I remember after I found out about Graham's affair, and how I hated him but couldn't let on. That first winter, as I recovered from my illness, I was simmering with resentment and it felt like everywhere I went, there he was. I took comfort in cooking and when he got back from work I would escape into the kitchen, leaving him with the children and a less than subtle hint that it was his turn now. But even then he'd arrive at my side, sooner or later. He was in pieces, and looking for reassurance – that I was getting better (I was), and that I didn't know about his affair (I did). I had no wish to reassure him, and if it hadn't been for the children I might have left him. He had broken my heart.

But that feels so long ago now, and I look back at that younger me and see how much I needed to learn about life. And that Graham was stupid but not the absolutely evil, heartless creature I had him pegged as for a while.

This evening, I find myself telling Teresa and Kiran about it all, though I know I have told them the story before. But I suppose with the wedding anniversary coming up, my marriage is at the fore of my mind and I'm keen to reflect on it.

"I am quite sure that H cheated on me, and more than once," says Teresa. "I suspect it was part and parcel of his entitled life. He certainly considered himself a bit of a ladies' man and a charmer. The worst thing is, it seemed to work. I suppose I felt a bit like you at first Ruth, but I just accepted it. At least it got him out of the house and away from me and Derek."

We watch the birds flitting between the branches of the oak, which is just beginning to green. Kiran doesn't give much away about her own marriage but

I get the feeling that, like her, it was quiet, calm and content.

"I think that's it," I say, remembering the moment I realised I no longer hated Graham. "You know how women talk, and discuss their relationships, and over time, at work and in my friendship group, I realised how different each one is. And that while Graham's actions had gutted me – it actually felt like he really had gutted me for a while – I came to see that he was a good husband in many ways. He stepped in when I was ill – no, no, I know–" I can see what Teresa is about to say – "he was only doing what he should have done, as a husband and a father, but we all know that is not always the case."

It's true; some of my friends had terrible husbands, who were out all the time, or who tried to control what their wives did, or who had to be asked for permission to go out. Graham was never like that. It made me begin to appreciate him again. I have a friend whose husband left her while she was having treatment for cancer, and their children were still teenagers. He couldn't cope, he said, and I am sure he may have been having a terrible time with his mental health but it still felt very much like 'so what'?

So while my feelings healed and I no longer hated Graham; in fact, over time I came to love him again, I never felt the same way about him as I had at the start. I'd been head over heels in love. I'd have done anything for him. That was no longer the case; but I do think now that maybe that wasn't such a bad thing. Why pin so much on one person?

"You let your friendships come back stronger," Kiran observes.

"Yes. I did. And I prioritised them in a way I might not have done, if Graham hadn't cheated on me, or if I had never found out."

"Friendships are not to be underestimated," Teresa nudges me.

"Oh, I know. Really, I know. And I'm so grateful for you two now. And the others." We are quite a community here, at the barrow.

"Isn't it lovely to be in this place; to have it to come back to? And to know that we all understand." Teresa smiles at me and Kiran.

A heron takes off from the waterlogged field on the other side of the oak tree, rising smoothly into the sky. It seems incredible that such a bird can actually move through the air like that; its shape seems so ungainly and awkward but we all grow quiet as it passes above us, heading to who knows where.

"Tom would have liked that," I say.

"Ah yes, your lovely boy! He and Kitty and Cecily were here earlier; Graham, too," says Teresa.

"Funny, Tom remarked that it felt like you weren't here," says Kiran. "He took your urn outside like he normally does but I could see that he didn't feel quite right."

"That is interesting," I say. Tom is the one who refers

to my ashes as 'Mum' whereas Annie and Kitty find that a bit uncomfortable. I'm with them, to be honest. The urn, the niche, the ashes… they are all representative of me, and I am very grateful for them. They mark my place on earth and remind people of my existence. And they form a focal point for my grieving family and friends. But maybe I underestimated Tom in thinking he was just trying to normalise my death and illustrate his acceptance of it. Maybe he does know more than I thought, and he really does feel my presence here.

"He's perceptive," Teresa nods. "As is Cecily. She's probably bringing that out in him."

"They're a lovely couple, aren't they?" I ask, half proudly, half shyly.

"Oh they are," says Kiran. "So lovely."

"I suppose if I hadn't… if I hadn't died, they wouldn't have met?" I try bravely, though that thought is actually upsetting.

"I don't think it's like that at all. I am sure that it would have happened between them, whatever. You know when you just think people are destined to meet?" Kiran says, smiling. "You didn't have to sacrifice yourself so your son could meet the love of his life. Those things are separate." It makes me feel better somehow. I would never want to get in the way of Tom meeting the love of his life, if that is what Cecily is, but I feel so sad at the thought of him living without me.

We were always close. I always hoped he'd meet a girl I liked and who would like me. I didn't want one of those awkward in-law relationships like Annie and Celia have. I was determined I'd be open and welcoming and remember what it is like to come into a family.

But I never got to try it out and see if I really could be the amazing person I hoped I could. And I miss Tom and how he'd sometimes still lean on me when he allowed himself to. And the way I could sometimes still make him laugh even when he didn't feel like it, and I'd see a glimpse of the little boy I once knew.

7

It's Wednesday evening and I'm in Annie's car with her, singing silently to the baby growing inside her, which wriggles a little and giggles, making Annie shift uncomfortably but also making her smile.

After a long day at the office, Annie doesn't feel like going home to be on her own. Neither does she feel like going round to Graham's, even if Tom is there – which he isn't. I happen to know he is round at Cecily's, charming her mum. He's a big hit with both of Cecily's parents and it makes me feel proud. Long may it last.

No, for Annie, there is only one person who is going to do tonight. Her sister.

She hums to herself as she drives, then she switches on the radio to listen to the news but it is, predictably, grim.

She switches it off again. Even realist Annie hasn't got the constitution for so much doom and gloom tonight. She's feeling down enough already. As she pulls into Kitty's street she can't see her sister's car and she kicks herself. She should have phoned first.

But hadn't Kitty said to just come over whenever she felt like it? Annie being Annie, she had taken that offer very much at face value. What if she's come all this way only to have to turn round and head home again? And she's dying for a wee as well. As usual. This baby is really taking over her life. But at least that sickness has died away. As quickly as it came, it's gone, and it's left her ravenous. Maybe she can stop at a McDonald's on the way back – use the loo and fill the gap with a burger or two. Nobody need know, she consoles herself. Because, I am sure it won't surprise you to know, Annie is very much Anti McDonald's.

But as she drives past the house which contains Kitty's flat, she sees a light is on and breathes a sigh of relief. There are so many cars on this road, Kitty must have ended up parking on a different street.

Annie, though, is lucky, and spies a space just big enough for her car. Efficiently and without a fuss, she reverses into it with a confidence I could have only dreamed of when I was alive. I would have been back and forth into that space, and almost certainly ended up driving off to find something a bit more spacious but streets away.

Switching off the engine, Annie feels the pressure on her bladder increase, as though her body is already relaxing now it knows that relief is not far away. She grabs her bag from the passenger seat and hurries across the street, ringing the doorbell with her sister's name underneath it, hoping that Kitty is quick to answer.

Footsteps, and a shape behind the door. Oh my god, she's going to wet herself. *Come on, Kitty. Why all the fiddling around?*

The door opens.

"Meg!"

"Annie!" Kitty's boss looks surprised, especially when Annie shoves her aside, muttering, "Anne." It's only the people closest to her that Annie will allow to call her the affectionate version of her name, and even then I'm not sure she's 100% comfortable with it.

Meg follows Annie up the stairs, a slightly amused look on her face that I'm glad Annie can't see. She closes the flat door and waits, hearing Annie sigh loudly and involuntarily from behind the bathroom door. The toilet flushes, the taps run, and Annie emerges ad heads into the lounge.

"What are you doing here?" she asks rudely and I wince. "Where's Kitty?"

Meg doesn't bat an eyelid though. "She's at the kennels. She's given me the night off, bless her."

"Damn. I wouldn't have come if I'd known you were here," Annie huffs.

"None taken!" Meg laughs. "I take it Kitty didn't know you were coming?"

"Obviously not."

"No worries. I'll give her a bell, relieve her of her duties."

"Haven't you just run that bath though?" Despite her preoccupation, Annie had noticed the tub full of bubbles, the steamed-up mirror. The candle, and the lone glass of wine on the windowsill.

"Yeah, it doesn't matter." Meg is used to things not going her way. If she ever – which is rarely – stops for a cup of tea or, god forbid, to actually try and read a book, the phone will go, or one of the dogs will start crying, or somebody will just arrive with a dog they no longer have time/space/patience/enthusiasm for. Sometimes she wonders if somewhere along the line somebody has put a curse on her. "No rest for the wicked," she will mutter, though Meg is far from wicked.

"Don't be stupid," Annie says. Rude, but not unkindly meant. "This is your night off. Kitty said she'd been trying to get you to take a break. And, no offence, but a bath might do you some good."

"You don't pull your punches do you?" Meg laughs again. She gingerly sniffs the arm of her sweatshirt. "I guess I do smell a bit doggy."

"Well you do spend all of your time with dogs."

"True."

"So go on, have your bath. I'll just have a cup of tea and I'll head back. I can come and see Kitty another night."

"You sure?"

"Of course. Take some time for yourself."

Meg shrugs and smiles, having been well apprised of Kitty's sister's 'quirks'. She knows Annie is a good person. God, she'd forgiven her sister for kissing her husband, surprisingly easily.

"Let me make you a drink first," she says. "You look tired."

"Do I?" asks Annie.

"A bit, yeah. I mean, you look great as well. Really. Being pregnant suits you. But I'm guessing you've been at work all day, and you must have driven straight over here. And have you eaten?"

"No," admits Annie, thoughts of that illicit McDonald's drifting back into her mind.

"Well look, if you're sure you don't want me to get Kitty back here, why don't you at least stay for some tea? I was going to treat myself to a takeaway."

Annie practically salivates at the word 'takeaway'. Meg sees this. "Come on, sit down for a bit. I'll put the kettle on."

"Alright," Annie concedes. "I am quite tired actually."

"Great. Tea?"

"Yes please. I've brough my own bags though." Annie fishes a ginger tea sachet from her handbag. She's still not confident she can stomach normal tea again.

Meg takes it from her and gently puts her hand on Annie's shoulder, pressing ever so slightly. Annie obediently sits down. Meg is used to dealing with recalcitrant dogs and she's taking a similar approach to Annie. Gentle, kind, and patient. Surely that just works for anyone, she thinks. Dog or human.

She pads through to the kitchen, enjoying being able to walk barefoot indoors without having to dodge the piles of fur that gather in the corners of her own living quarters. Putting on the kettle, she whistles to herself while the water boils, and smiles at the thought of Annie.

"Thank you," Annie says sincerely when Meg brings through a small pot with the ginger tea brewing inside, and a cup and saucer on a tray. There is a further saucer with a couple of ginger cookies on it.

"No worries." Meg smiles and beats a retreat to the bathroom, where her long-yearned-for bath awaits. She strips off her clothes, noting that Annie's right, she really does smell of dog. And acknowledging that it is not surprising, and it's entirely unavoidable. Even so, it is exceedingly sweet to slip through the bubbles into the steaming water and feel the heat on her skin, soaking through to her aching muscles. Meg rolls her shoulders, feeling a few little creaks and clicks. She closes her eyes, slides back until the water is up to her chin, and she moans ever so slightly. It's been a long time since she has experienced anything much in the way of physical pleasure. I leave her to it.

Annie, I discover, has not stayed seated for long. Instead, nosy older sister that she is, after eating both the cookies, she has walked through to Kitty's spare room, which doubles as her art studio. Entirely lacking in respect for Kitty's privacy, she lifts covers from a couple of works in progress – a large landscape of the long barrow, the other a small but labour-intensive portrait of me. Annie gasps at the sight of this one. It is really lovely, I have to admit, and an extremely flattering depiction of what I actually looked like. With soft light and my eyes half-closed, like I am looking at something on the ground, this picture is destined for Graham, for a wedding anniversary present perhaps, if Kitty deems it is the right thing to do at the time. She's unsure if it will just set him off on another journey of misery and grief.

Annie replaces the cover carefully then spends more time looking at the long barrow painting. This is one of a series, she knows, and it is stunning. It's not her usual taste, being a very bold and bright, modern take on a landscape, but there is something about it that she's drawn to. She stands and considers it for some time, wondering whether Kitty would be pleased to receive a message praising her, or annoyed that her big sister is snooping. Annoyed, probably. She carefully replaces the cover over this picture too, and exits the room, switching off the light as she goes.

All is quiet in the bathroom and Annie has no wish to disturb Meg during her luxurious bath. Instead, she sits back down and pours a cup of tea. She sips it slowly then replaces it on the saucer and leans her head back against the cushion. Her eyes begin to close.

No, Annie, she tells herself. *Do not doze off now*. She stands and shakes her head, as if trying to expel her fatigue. Wanders over to the bathroom door.

"Meg?" she asks tentatively.

"Yes?" Meg calls back. "Is everything OK? Do you need the loo?"

"Oh yeah, I mean no. Everything's fine but I don't need the bathroom. I just thought maybe I could order the takeaway so it might be here when you get out of the bath. I mean, no rush." She coughs awkwardly, practising the kind of thing I might have said to Meg in this situation. No rush. Though actually those cookies have barely touched the sides. Annie is incredibly hungry. Her mind drifts back to the dream she'd had, of me and her in Italy, me offering her an olive. She'd love an olive now. A whole jar of them...

"Great idea. Thanks, Anne. I'll give you some cash when I'm out of here."

"Don't worry about that," Annie says, again channelling me, or Kitty, or Tom. Thinking how she'd like to be better at putting people at ease. Like this is no big deal that she's in her sister's flat, with her sister's boss, but without her sister. Ordering an off-the-cuff takeaway. Maybe she can just act like she's relaxed and at least convince Meg, if not herself.

"OK, thanks. Chinese?"

"Yes. I like Chinese." *Not natural enough*, she chides herself. "Any preference? Allergies?"

"I'm vegetarian," Meg reminds her.

"Of course." Annie had actually assumed this, knowing Kitty's commitment to the cause and assuming her boss would be the same.

"But don't let that stop you," Meg calls.

"I'll sort it," says Annie. And she does. She orders a vegetarian banquet for two, and by the time Meg has emerged from the bathroom, in pyjamas and with a towel wrapped around her hair, Annie has set the small dining table with plates, bowls, spoons, forks, chopsticks, and even poured a fresh glass of wine for Meg.

"Wow!" Meg exclaims. "This is great!"

"Well Kitty's told me how hard you work. And how much you need a break. This is… it's not much but hopefully it's OK."

"It's lovely, Anne. Really."

Annie blushes and smiles slightly. She doesn't know what to say and she's relieved that the doorbell goes. "That'll be the food," she says.

"Hey, I'll go," Meg protests. "You've done all this, and you're…"

"Pregnant, not an invalid," Annie says firmly.

Meg laughs. "I am sure I'd say exactly the same," she admits.

They look at each other and recognise shared ground. And by the time Annie has brought the carrier bags upstairs, Meg is sitting with her damp hair loose around her shoulders, sipping her wine. Allowing herself to be looked after. Just a little bit. Just this once.

"So what's Kitty like, to work with?" Annie asks. She's been scraping around her mind for some suitable topics of conversation. Remembered the thing I told her about the weather – we often gravitate towards it as a subject because it's common ground. She does not wish to discuss the weather now but can't see much in the way of commonality with Meg. Except, of course, Kitty.

"Oh she's so great!" Meg says. "She's a friend as much as anything. Above everything."

"I don't really have any friends at work," Annie says, surprising herself but not, apparently Meg. Why is that? Is it so obvious that people won't want to be friends with Annie?

"Ah, but you're the boss, aren't you?"

"So are you," Annie shoots back.

"Well, yes, but you work in a different world to me. It's more…"

"Corporate?"

"I was going to say *male*."

Annie smiles, her eyes meeting Meg's. "It is male. Incredibly so."

"I would imagine that to have achieved everything you have, you've had to keep a little bit apart from your colleagues." Meg is being kind, knowing Annie is not the most socially at ease person, but there is truth in this.

"Yes, but fat lot of good it's done me. Now I'm pregnant."

"Oh?"

And Annie finds herself telling Meg about Jeff, and Ryan Edwards.

"So they're just replacing you?" Meg is outraged. "Because you're having a baby?"

"It looks like it," sniffs Annie. "Though I'm going to try my utmost to avoid that happening." And she explains her plan to Meg, who listens, carefully and sympathetically. Annie notices the intelligence in Meg's face, and the earnestness with which she pays attention.

"Why put yourself through all that?" Meg asks.

"Because I've worked damn hard to get where I am," Annie snaps.

Meg, calm and unaffected by the brusque reply, says, "Well yes, I can see that. I'm not saying stop working. I'm saying maybe it's time to do things differently."

"In what way?" Annie asks.

"Hear me out." Meg pours herself a third glass of wine and takes a sip. "I think you should leave your job."

Just those words are enough to create a flurry of panic in my daughter. I try to soothe her; pass the message on to her own daughter within her. *Calm*, I say, I whisper. *Be calm. And listen.* Because I think what Meg is about to say is worth listening to.

"I haven't always run a kennels," Meg says.

"No?" Annie isn't really interested, too preoccupied with the thought of not having her job anymore and what that would mean to her.

"No. I was. Well, I was a bit like you."

I doubt it, Annie thinks, but she is intrigued.

"I went to uni, and I did business and marketing. I loved it. And I was full of drive, and passion. I had a boyfriend who I'd met when I was at sixth form and I was so eager to begin our grown-up life together. I didn't make loads of friends at university and I lived at home because, well because it was cheaper, so I didn't really get into the whole social side of things."

"Nor me," says Annie, and both are aware that it wasn't for lack of funds.

"I threw myself into my work. And when I wasn't working, I was applying to businesses for post-grad schemes. Fast-tracks to success."

"Really?" Annie's attention is all Meg's now.

"Really. And I got offered a place, with a big IT company in Birmingham. I got a high 2:1 as well but I was gutted that it wasn't a first."

"I had no idea about this," Annie says.

"No, well I don't talk about it much. It wasn't a very happy time in my life. My god, I was so excited to start work, and move to my own place. I rented a flat on the outskirts of Birmingham and I could get the train to work in the morning. I felt so grown-up, in my work clothes, slotting into a carriage between all the other workers heading into the city to do great things."

"And the reality…?"

"Well, it began well. There was an induction period for the graduates – I was one of six, and the only girl – and that was great. People were mostly nice and welcoming. But it was exhausting, and my boyfriend back home decided I wasn't paying enough attention to him, so he dumped me."

Annie rolls her eyes.

"I know!" laughs Meg. "I think I'd outgrown him anyway. And actually, we're friends again now. But back then I was sad, but it just made me all the more determined to do well. And once the settling-in period was over, I was placed in a team whose job it was to write bids, and try to win new clients – and retain existing ones."

"That's not easy," sympathises Annie.

"No, and it was hard, long hours. Some of my colleagues thrived on it I suppose; it felt like it was an excuse to stay away from home, for a couple of them."

"Men?" Annie asks.

"Oh yeah. I was the only woman."

"Ouch."

"Exactly. A sole – very young – female, in a fast-moving, highly competitive and incredibly corporate world. There was a lot of socialising with clients too and, slightly green around the gills, I was shocked at the attention I got from men. Older, often married, men."

"And I'm guessing it wasn't your professional skills they were interested in?"

"No," Meg says dejectedly. "I don't think they could give a toss about how good I was at my job. Honestly, it was grim. But also… I had a crush. On one of my colleagues."

"Oh no. Don't tell me…"

"Yes, he was married. With kids. But – *his wife didn't understand him.*"

Both Annie and Meg grin knowingly.

"And we were together, for years. Nearly four of them. I mean – not together, as such. Because he was married, and had a family. But if there was ever the prospect of a night away, we'd both jump at the chance. My god, I was an idiot. And, I haven't really told many people about this. I'm too embarrassed, to be honest. I normally just tell people I was with somebody who didn't like dogs, and that's enough to convince them! But really, I liked this guy a lot. He kept saying he'd leave his wife for me, when the time was right. He said he loved me." She flushes at the memory. "I was so dumb!"

"And your career...?" Annie asks, spearing a piece of mushroom with a chopstick.

"Yeah, well, it probably wasn't my brightest move, hooking up with one of my married colleagues. People knew, of course, and the other women in the office were pretty awful, while the men kind of liked the idea and also liked to make jokes, usually at my expense. But I carried on working, and I moved on to a better job, with really amazing pay for somebody my age, and the hours and responsibility to go with it. So I do know, Anne, what it's like to be all about work."

Meg brings the conversation back round to Annie. But she is not ready to move back to herself just yet.

"So what happened?" Annie asks, pouring seaweed liberally over her second helping of Szechuan vegetables and noodles. She is so hungry.

"Oh, it just... it fizzled out."

"With the man?"

"Yes. Nothing major. No dramatics. I suppose I grew a bit more demanding, and started to think that maybe he wasn't intending to leave his wife after all."

"Surprise!" says Annie and Meg grins ruefully.

"Ha! Yeah. What a shocker. And after that, work was awkward. I started to realise what an idiot I'd been, and what a reputation I'd managed to make for myself."

"But you didn't do anything wrong."

"Well, yes and no. I did have an affair with a married man. A colleague."

"Yes, but he was the one who was married!" Annie exclaims indignantly.

"I know, and I agree. I really do. If I was to look at that situation from the outside I'd see it the way you do, I am sure. But at the same time I knew it was wrong and I felt really guilty. And ashamed. It began to affect my work, and to affect how I felt about myself. And in the end, I had a breakdown. All before the age of thirty."

"Oh," Annie breathes. "I really had no idea, Meg." She looks at the woman across the table from her and feels like she is seeing her so differently. That Meg even looks different to how she did.

"Yeah. It wasn't pretty. I took time off work, for mental health reasons, which is something I had never, ever wanted to do. But my parents came to my rescue, my mum in particular. She helped me sort my head out. It was hard for them, seeing the way I'd gone, and how obsessed I'd become with work. How withdrawn I was from anything outside of it. They didn't know about the man, although I think Mum had her suspicions. She took me home, and she looked after me, and she found me a counsellor, and I felt safe, but I felt like a failure."

"Oh that's bad," Annie says. It's not easy for her to put herself in somebody else's shoes but she is giving it her best shot. I'm proud of her.

"Yeah. Well, after that I couldn't go back to the office, could I? There was no way. And thankfully for me, there was a round of redundancies, and the company was more than happy to absolve itself of any responsibility towards me, and it cleaved me away. I sold my flat, and I stayed at home for another year, while my little brother went the opposite way, moving out to live with his girlfriend. He's six years younger than me and you might be able to imagine that just added to my sense of worthlessness. I felt like such a failure."

"Urgh, that's awful," Annie says, trying to put all of this together in her mind. Seeing how, yes, it might make one feel worse if they had come back home with their tail between their legs, only to see their younger sibling moving on and out into the world. To be living at home when you'd found and made your independence.

"But it was all for the best. Sorry, I didn't mean to make this all about me. It was meant to be about you!" Meg laughs. "Because what I did, when I was back on my feet again, was use my redundancy money, and the money I'd made from selling my flat, to help get the kennels. And I wrote a business case and got a loan from the bank."

"I don't think I want to run a kennels," Annie said politely, not wishing to cause offence, and being incredibly dense. I can see what Meg is saying and I'm thinking, *Yes!*

"That is definitely not what I'm saying!" Meg laughs. "I also don't think you should run a kennels. But do you know what you should do?"

"What?"

"Strike out on your own."

"On my own?"

"Yes! You're good, Annie. You must be, very good, at what you do. Kitty is so in awe of you."

"Is she?" Annie feels pleased at this thought.

"Of course she is! Bloody hell Anne, she talks about you all the time. She's so proud of you."

"I had no idea."

"Well, she should tell you." The fourth glass of wine is taking effect and Meg's mouth is thoroughly lubricated now. The words are slipping out unchecked, aided by emotion and passion and a sense of righteousness. "And you, Anne, you should stop and look back at what you've achieved. You're always looking ahead, I think, and you need to give yourself a moment to appreciate what you've done so far."

"I..."

"Really!" The awareness of being wronged in her own working life (she's checked LinkedIn, seen her old 'love' has now pushed his way to the top rung of the corporate ladder, though he's not looking so good on it) is fuelling Meg's enthusiasm. Somebody's got to benefit from it, she thinks. And here is Annie; straight-laced, serious, and sometimes baffled by the world. Meg can see it, and she also knows what happened with Kitty and Alex, and she's absolutely blown away by Annie's take on that.

My daughter is not 'normal' and Meg sees that but she doesn't perceive it as a negative. This, she thinks, could very well be Annie's super-power.

"Fucking hell, Anne, do you really want to sit around and watch everything you've worked for be kicked apart by this... Richard?"

"Ryan," Annie corrects. "And no, I don't."

"And will your boss have your back? While you're on maternity leave?"

Annie remembers the sound of the male laughter resounding round the empty office at the weekend.

"No, I don't expect he will."

"So does he deserve your loyalty?"

"No," Annie realises.

"And look, you're going to have a baby. I mean, I am no expert, but it's going to change your life. The responsibility! I mean, I have responsibility for, like, fifteen dogs at a time, and it's huge. But a real, helpless human being…? It's got to be another step on. I don't know. Unless your ex is going to do his fair share and more, there will be times you're conflicted. Work will need you and the baby will have a temperature or something."

A tiny flare of panic in my daughter.

"It's OK, Anne," Meg has seen the slight widening of eyes. "It's normal. But it will happen. And where will you want to be? At work, trying to fight Richard away from your precious job?"

"I just, I assumed I'd work it out. Get a childminder…"

"You could do that," agrees Meg. "But honestly, striking out on my own has been the best thing I've ever done. Yes, I might smell like dogs a lot of the time. OK, all of the time. And yes, as your sister has noticed, there are times I'm struggling with finances, and I have been known to sleep in the office. But oh, the relief of not having to try and please other people all the time, or suck up to idiots, or put up with the sexist 'banter' that I hated so bloody much. *We're just having a laugh, Meg. Don't take it so seriously.* Urgh."

Annie eyes Meg carefully. She is drunk, that's in no doubt, and yet, she is speaking to something in Annie. There is some sense in her words. Even so, my Annie is not one for rash decisions, or for being talked into something by somebody else. Any decision she makes will have to be hers alone. But she can't deny that Meg has given her something to think about. And she also can't deny that Kitty's boss is full of surprises and, what's more, she's really good company. And easy to talk to.

Annie looks at Meg. Takes a deep breath. Decides to tell her what she'd come here to talk to Kitty about.

"It's not just work, Meg," Annie says.

"No?"

"No. It's Alex. My ex. He's met somebody else."

8

This is what Alex had wanted to talk to Annie about the other day but even Alex – not always the most emotionally mature of men – had realised that Annie was not in the right frame of mind on Sunday to hear this news. But he did not want to leave it too long. In part because he felt uncomfortable keeping it a secret but also, if he is honest, just a very small part of him wanted to feel like he had the upper hand. Because, despite everything – the fact that he had been the one to kiss his wife's sister, for example – Alex has felt very much like Annie's been the driving force in their splitting up, much as she has been throughout their relationship. In fact, if he is very honest, Alex wonders if Annie was pleased when she found out about him and Kitty. If it provided her with the reason she'd been looking for to put an end to things between them.

But no, I know that she was in fact very hurt. That the incident on New Year's Eve was not only a betrayal but also confirmed to her something she has always known, about her inability to connect with people in the same way that most of her family and friends and colleagues can. Of course Alex would prefer Kitty to her, she thought. Lovely, bright, sunny Kitty. Kind Kitty. Beautiful, creative and thoughtful Kitty. Annie loves her sister for all of these things as well but throughout their lives she has become increasingly aware of the difference between who Kitty is and how she sees the world, and treats people, to who she, Annie, is and how she behaves.

So in a way it didn't surprise her that Alex liked her sister, though she found it more difficult to see what the attraction might be for Kitty. And she retreated for a while, thinking it through, switching on her rational mind to work through what had happened and why, and what it meant for her. And I am so proud of her that she could do that, and come out the other side so sensibly and proportionally, and that she and Kitty are back to how they always were. A more emotional person may not have been able to get to this point and I want so much to tell Annie that. To let her know that how she is may make life harder but also enables her to be different in such a good way.

Alex fails to see all this, for he is cradling his own hurt too. That throughout his relationship with Annie, she never gave him what he wanted; the reassurance, the stability, of feeling loved and wanted. They were not unhappy together but neither could quite meet the other's needs. Still, they both care about the other and Alex is keen to prove his worth in supporting her through this pregnancy and beyond. He is determined to be a good father and he's determined that Annie will let him be. But also, now, well… Donna.

She and Alex work together, and have done for some time. Donna is six years younger than Alex, and in fact was at school with Tom, though Alex hasn't realised that yet. Donna laughs at his jokes and she sees the best side of Alex. The way he listens to other people in meetings, and goes out of his way to make sure that every voice is heard, including hers. Early on in her working life, she'd been very shy and quiet and barely able to speak when it came to project meetings, but Alex had seen this, and had subtly opened the way for her to offer her thoughts, smiling encouragingly at her and following her stilted words with a positive, "I think Donna's made a very valid point there," and following it with his own thoughts, moving the attention of their colleagues swiftly on from Donna herself and giving her a chance to breathe and calm her shakiness down.

She had always been grateful to Alex for that moment, and over the years they'd worked closely together, and gravitated towards each other at work social events but, Alex had told himself, there was never anything in it. Donna was herself in a relationship and he, of course, was an older married man. He felt a bit as he did about Kitty towards Donna, like she was a younger sister. But look how it had gone with Kitty. And now, things with Donna had followed suit.

Life was never straightforward, though, Alex thought. Not now he was older. When he and Annie had got together, they were young and had nothing in the way of baggage. It had been a simple matter of him asking her out, planning a lovely romantic date, kissing her – that had been the most nerve-racking part – and falling into the habit of spending as much time as possible together, meeting each other's parents, moving in together… all leading quite obviously to his eventual proposal and Annie's acceptance. When Alex looks back now, he wonders if he ever stopped to think if he was actually, really, happy. But he loved Annie; was awed by her. He couldn't bear the thought of life without her. It's only now that he really understands that she never made him feel good about himself. Not in the way that Donna does.

"Annie, I have to tell you something," he said on the phone at lunchtime.

"OK," she had said, sitting in her car in the work car park, watching a small crew of sparrows mess about in the hedgerow, flitting to and fro and twittering at each other in loud voices.

"I've met somebody." Alex just came out with it, feeling proud of himself for his honesty and forthrightness.

"Oh?" The level of disinterest in Annie's voice was cutting.

"Yes," he pressed on. "I – I thought I should tell you. I thought you had a right to know."

"OK, thanks Alex." God, she can come across as cold, my daughter. Only I, sitting in her passenger seat, can see the dismay on her face. Annie is grateful that she is hearing this news via phone; that she does not have to rearrange her features to match her tone of voice.

"She's – it's – somebody at work."

"Donna?" Annie is quick and sharp and, though she hasn't necessarily consciously considered this before, she was often aware of how much Alex would talk about Donna. It had irritated her, but never worried her. She is not the jealous type, she thinks, but I think she has just not yet met the person who could bring out jealousy in her.

"Yes. How did – how did you know?"

"Just a feeling," Annie says, her mouth a straight line.

"But it's a new thing, Annie," Alex says. "Like, nothing's really happened yet anyway."

"You haven't slept with her?" Her bluntness is wonderful sometimes, I think.

"I – no, I... it's none of your business," he finishes with a flourish of something like strength, realising that it really is not Annie's place to ask that question. But she has already wrong-footed him with her words.

"So what is going on, then?"

"We've been spending time together." They've been to the cinema, out for a couple of meals. They were spending lunchtimes together, most days, which of course had not escaped their colleagues' attention.

"Annie and I are splitting up," Alex had told Donna glumly one grey spring day, while rained poured from the sky outside, battering the windows, and Alex had taken a sad bite of his unsatisfying sandwich, pale and wilting.

"Joel and I have broken up too," Donna said, pushing her home-made pasta salad around its plastic container.

The two colleagues had looked at each other then, their eyes meeting in the glow of the too-bright lighting. And something had brightened a little for them both; who had been nursing their – if not broken hearts – their fragile egos and a sense of disappointment in life.

Alex had smiled but quickly recovered himself. "Are you OK?" he asked.

"Yeah, I – I think so. It's been coming for a long time, if I'm honest."

"Same," said Alex.

And Donna had smiled at him, but they had returned to their lunches and their own thoughts, and eventually to their own desks, feeling just a little bit better about life, each aware of this tiny window of possibility that had just opened up.

Even so, it had taken a while for anything to happen. Alex was still trying to keep his options open with

Annie. He likes to think that he takes the concept of marriage very seriously and remembers the vows he made to her. When she eventually told him about the baby, he was ready to do everything he could to patch things up. Only she wouldn't let him. She didn't want him to. She didn't want him.

And over the weeks he's found himself opening up to Donna; laying bare his sadness and disappointment, and fears, that Annie won't let him be involved with the child as much as he'd like. And Donna, steadfast and loyal to this man who has helped her come out of herself at work, has reacted with sympathy and indignation.

"But you're the dad," she said. "No matter what's happened between you two–" Alex has omitted the detail about him kissing Kitty – "she can't keep you out of your baby's life."

"I know," said Alex, "and, to be fair to Annie, I don't really think she would. But now we don't live together, it's difficult, to feel part of anything…"

"Oh Alex," Donna had laid a soft hand on his arm and he'd looked at her, and both had felt something as their eyes had met. And on the Friday night of that week, they'd left the office at the same time, not entirely – or even at all – by accident, and she'd asked him if he'd like to go out for something to eat, and so they had, Alex phoning Celia to say he wouldn't be home for tea ("You could have told me earlier," she'd huffed). They'd talked non-stop over their meal, and had a couple of drinks at a local bar, and then Alex had put Donna in a taxi, and just before she'd gone in, he'd caught her hand, and he'd kissed her.

"Alright?" he'd smiled softly and her answering beam had confirmed that yes, it was more than alright, and ever since then they'd been trying to hide their glances across the office, and the spring in their steps, swapping clandestine messages and talking long into the night. And things really haven't progressed physically from more than a short kiss, but they are progressing, and Alex had wanted Annie to know. And now she does.

"Well, thanks for telling me," Annie said, eyes still on the sparrows, one hand on her belly.

"Annie, I—"

She hung up.

And she sat, for some time, just watching the birds, stroking her stomach, thinking of the tiny being in there that she and Alex had made together – not deliberately, but together nonetheless – and knowing that there was no going back now. Realising that she wouldn't want to.

And then she got to thinking that this time last year I was still around. We had known of my illness by this point and in fact I would have been on my third round of treatment, the one that hit me hardest. But I'd have been her first port of call and I'd have wanted to be, too. Annie knew that on hearing this news from Alex, she would have called me. Maybe not immediately, but it wouldn't have been long before she would have let me know, wanting to hear what my thoughts were; hoping to take some advice from me, about how to go forward.

In putting the phone down on Alex, she wasn't expressing her unhappiness or disapproval; she was just giving herself the chance to stop and think before saying anything else. Alex, of course, took it as a gesture of anger but then, as we know, he's never really, truly understood Annie. No matter how long they've known each other.

"Mum," she said into the empty space of her car, and it was close to a wail. My loss, my absence, kicking her hard once more, as grief tends to do, returning swiftly and sharply just when you think you've tamed it and got it under control. "Oh, Mum."

And I reached out, wanting to tuck that little strand of hair behind her ear. Yearning to hold her, and comfort her, and tell her everything was going to be alright. But she didn't feel me; had no idea I was there. And she sat instead, for the rest of her lunchbreak, feeling utterly alone.

But just before it was time to return to her desk, and her responsibility, and she was trying to pull her professional face back on, Annie's phone beeped. It was Kitty. She was just sending a photo of one of the rescue dogs to the family WhatsApp group, but it reminded Annie that, despite everything, she was not alone in the world, and that there was somebody else who loved her and cared about her, and who may not be me but was the next best thing.

9

After Annie and Meg cleared away the takeaway dishes, they moved to Kitty's sofa, which has seen better days but is supremely comfortable. Annie could see Meg was tired – and, yes, a little drunk – and their conversation began to take a more leisurely turn. Meg had already expressed her feelings about Alex, having previously heard Kitty's side of the New Year's Kiss story. It's fair to say she doesn't have the highest opinion of Annie's estranged husband.

"He's not so bad," Annie surprises herself by saying as she sits at one end of the seat, her legs curled up and a cushion pulled onto her lap.

"Who?" Meg asks softly.

"Alex. I know, I know, he sounds like a right…. twat." Anie, who rarely swears, feels daring calling him that. Meg can see this and smiles slightly. "But you know, I haven't been the nicest wife. Honestly–" before Meg can protest – "really. He needs something, Alex, which I can't give him."

"A kick up the arse?"

That has them both laughing.

"But no, really. Alex is somebody who needs… reassurance. Affection."

"Love?" Meg asks, adroitly.

Annie looks at her. "I do – did – love him."

"Yeah, I can see that you care about him. And love him. But is that the same as being in love with him?"

"I don't know what being in love means," Annie admits.

"No, to be fair, I'm not sure I really believe in it myself," Meg says. "Seems like an awful lot of hassle. I definitely used to be a believer. Now I just feel like relationships are a purely selfish thing. Like being 'in love' is just a way of trying to control somebody, own them – it's about what we get out of it. That intensity, and passion – it's a buzz, but it's not going to last. Sorry, I'm waffling now…"

Annie is quiet. Intensity. It's not a word she would use about Alex; not passion, either. Maybe she is entirely incapable of feeling those things. But no, she thinks. She does feel them when it comes to her work. She rolls her eyes, at herself. What kind of a robot is she?

Meg sees the eye-roll. "What?"

"Well I was just thinking, what you're describing. I don't think I've ever felt like that."

"Not even at the beginning, with Alex?"

"No. I— I suppose I just really liked him. He was kind, and I found him easy to talk to – which I don't always, with other people, you know…" Even admitting this is uncomfortable, and I'm proud of her.

"I liked the physical stuff too, most of the time. Less, as the years went on." They both laugh at this.

"Well I think that's normal. Not that I'm any kind of expert. But it sounds like there might have been something missing, you know. You should feel so happy to be with your partner. They should excite you. I know that's not realistic forever but I do think that's how it should be at the beginning. Then again, what do I know? Like I say, I'm not sure I really believe in the whole 'in love' thing these days."

"You're a cynic," observes Annie.

"I suppose," Meg says. She closes her eyes briefly. "And I'm a bit drunk."

"I'll get out of your hair soon," Annie says.

"What? No, you don't need to do that."

"I've taken up your entire evening."

"It's been good. Really good," says Meg, smiling. "Honestly."

"Didn't you want some time to yourself, though?"

"Listen, I have time to myself every night. Literally – every night. Having grown-up, human, company this evening has been really lovely. And you know, I think we have a lot in common."

"I think we do too," Annie smiles.

"I'm really glad that Kitty has you. I wish I had a sister like you," Meg says.

"Really?" Annie is genuinely taken aback by this. She's long been used to feeling like a bit of a millstone for her brother and sister.

"God, yeah! So down-to-earth and honest. And you forgave Kitty for…"

"There was nothing to forgive. Honestly."

"You're a lovely person, Anne."

"Call me Annie," my daughter smiles. I am surprised they don't hear my gasp. I am so proud of her right now.

"Annie," Meg smiles back. Her eyes flicker closed again.

"You're tired," Annie says. "I should go."

"You're not driving back at this time of night," Meg says. "I'll sleep here, and you have Kitty's bed."

"No! This is your night off, you should have the bed."

"Honestly, this is already a hundred times more comfortable than kipping in the office. You're the one with a bun in the oven. You have the bed."

Annie actually laughs. "If you're sure."

"I am. Trust me."

"Well I'll just go and get us both some water…"

"Lovely," Meg murmurs, already shuffling down a bit on the seat.

Annie goes to the little kitchen and runs the tap for a while, feeling rightly proud of herself. Friendship does not come easily to her but she's really enjoyed herself tonight. And Meg seems to – like her? Could that be?

It feels like somebody squeezing my heart when I realise what Annie is thinking. That she's so surprised that somebody actually likes her. That she has gone through over thirty years of life feeling like people tolerate her, but don't actually want to be friends with her or spend time with her. My eldest daughter has come to accept this about herself and just live with it. To the point that now she has realised somebody has enjoyed spending an evening in her company – just a simple evening in with a takeaway, which would be no big deal to most people – it feels like the greatest thing in the world.

"Here," she says, returning to the living room with two full pint glasses in hand. But Meg is fast asleep. Annie puts the drinks down and gently moves a small table closer to the sofa, but just far enough away that Meg won't knock it over in her sleep, then she puts one of the glasses on it and takes the other through to Kitty's room. She finds the spare duvet that Tom usually uses when he stays over, and takes it through to cover Meg up. Then, ever so quietly, Annie uses the little bathroom and makes her way through to the bed, climbing in fully clothed. She hadn't thought this visit through so she has no pyjamas, no toothbrush, no cleanser or moisturiser. But it's OK, she realises. For one night she can cope without them. As she slides further down under the covers, she thinks of that portrait of me that Kitty is working on, and her sudden tears surprise her. Then she sees on the bedside table a photo of Kitty and Meg, and a few of the dogs from the kennels, alongside a scrawled note from Kitty: *In case you're missing us. Woof woof.* Left for

Meg's benefit of course but it makes Annie smile. She switches off the light, thinking of her sister and her sister's boss, and feeling grateful that she has these people in her life.

"Annie… there's a cup of tea here."

It takes more than a few moments for Annie to work out where she is. "Kitty?"

"Yes, it's me! Meg couldn't sleep in and she turned up at the kennels at about half-five, and sent me home to see you."

"What time is it now?"

"It's about half-seven."

"Shit. I need to get to work." She sits up suddenly. "I have to get home and get changed. I'm going to be so late…"

"About that…"

"What?" Annie leans back on her elbows.

"I called in sick for you."

"You did *what?*"

"I phoned the office, thinking I'd get the answerphone, but somebody called Sam answered."

"You spoke to Sam?"

"Yes, he was lovely. He said you work too hard anyway and should take a day off to look after yourself."

Annie can't help but smile at this but inside, her heart is pounding. "I can't miss a day," she says. "It will only confirm my weakness."

"Weakness?" Kitty exclaims.

"Yes, you know – I'm pregnant, blah blah blah."

"Yes. You're pregnant. And you're as strong as a fucking ox."

"Then I need to be in work," Annie argues.

"No, you need to be looking out for yourself. Meg told me, about that guy taking your place."

"He hasn't taken my—"

"Annie," Kitty says, looking her sister in the eye. "We all know how things go. And Meg said you were thinking of going freelance?"

"Well, I don't know about…"

"Think about it!" Kitty urges. "That's why I called you in sick. You need to really think about it. Look into how it might work. That place is no good for you. Honestly. Bringing in some bloke to replace you while you're pregnant…" Kitty has righteous indignation burning through her veins right now. She hopes Annie won't mind that Meg has told her.

"It does… it does feel wrong." Annie takes a sip of the tea that Kitty has brought her and is relieved to find it tastes good. "I don't hate tea anymore!" she exclaims.

"You hated tea?"

"Only since I've been pregnant. It does strange things to you, honestly."

"Sorry, I should have asked what you actually wanted."

"Don't be sorry! It is lovely, having a cup of tea brought to me. And I had a good time last night, with Meg." Annie's speaking but inwardly thinking, can she really take the day off? Can she really risk her position at the company? She doesn't *do* sick days; she is like Graham in that respect, as she is in so many others.

But could she really branch out alone? And how would it really work? She will still have a baby, and that will have to come first.

"Dad will help, you know," says Kitty, as though reading her sister's mind. Pressing the advantage. "And Alex, of course. In fact, Alex won't be *helping*. He will be looking after his child, the same as what you'll be doing."

"He's got a girlfriend," Annie says.

"Who, Alex?" Kitty already knew this too but decided not to let on that Meg had told her absolutely everything.

"Yes." Annie finds she really doesn't mind. In fact, she thinks, it will be good for him. And alleviate some of the pressure on her.

"Well, he's one of them, isn't he?"

"One of what?"

"He can't be on his own. Some people are like that."

"Are they?"

"Yes, they need somebody else to validate them, and make them feel good about themselves."

"I'd say I failed fairly spectacularly in that respect.

Poor Alex."

"Poor Alex, my foot!" Kitty says, in what is a more than passable imitation of me. It makes them both laugh. "So will you do it? Think about it, at least?"

"What?"

"Branching out on your own."

"I don't know."

"But you will take the day off?"

"I think I have to, don't I? If you've already called in?"

"Great! You can come to the kennels if you want to. Come and see what I do."

"With all those smelly dogs?" But Annie is smiling.

"Yes, with all those smelly, lovely dogs. And Meg said she'd tell you a bit about being self-employed, if you'd like her to."

Oh my god. Is she really doing this? Thinking about it, at least? Annie checks herself. It appears that she is.

"Alright then. But can I have a shower first? And also after?" She actually grins.

"Of course! I'll dig out some of my old clothes for you to borrow." Kitty assesses Annie's current, crumpled, outfit, which she was wearing for work. She also sees the slightest, gentlest bump in Annie's tummy. It brings a lump to her throat.

She goes to her drawers and rummages through them for some comfortable trousers and a long-sleeved top. "What did you think of my pictures?" she asks, her back to her sister.

"Your…?"

"Come on Annie, I know you'll have looked at them!" laughs Kitty. "Two works in progress, with covers over them? Don't pretend you didn't take a peek… you wouldn't have been able to stop yourself!"

Annie actually blushes. "Well I, well, er… they're very good. I love the one of Mum."

"I knew it!" Kitty laughs. "Do you think Dad will like it?"

"He definitely will. It's beautiful."

"I thought I might bring it to London, give it to him while we're away. Is that a good idea?" "It's lovely, Kitty. Really lovely."

"Honestly?"

"Yes."

"Thank you, Annie. Now drink your tea, and then you can have a shower and get changed. It's Bring Your Sister to Work day."

"Thank you, Kitty," Annie says just before her sister leaves the room.

"What for?"

"Everything. All of this. I didn't realise I needed it, but it is very nice to feel looked after."

10

It's London Day! I feel nearly as excited as my family do about this trip. They squeeze onto a table for four on the train, every single one of them thinking that we never used to be able to all sit together. As a family of five it was often hard to make things fit and it used to annoy me; not that you can do much about the layout of a train, but family tickets always seemed to be for a family of four. Family rooms in hotel – made for four. Or they would be doubles and twins, meaning Tom as the youngest was often to be found on a fold-up bed in our room, the girls having protested about having him in with them but being too young (and it being too expensive) to have a room of his own. Of course I don't, or didn't, expect the world to shape itself to fit around my circumstances, it just felt sometimes though as if everything was set for the perfectly round-numbered nuclear family, and of course for most people life just isn't that neat.

"I should have upgraded to first class," Graham mutters, shuffling slightly uncomfortably.

"This is fine, Dad," says Tom, drawing out a box of

playing cards. He had actually hoped that Cecily might come along this weekend but she'd told him no.

"It's lovely of you to think of me but this is for your family," she had said firmly. "No, honestly, I wouldn't feel comfortable, and I think it's important that you all spend these firsts together. It'll be weird for your dad, his first wedding anniversary without your mum. Having you three around him will help enormously."

Instead, Cecily is staying at our house and looking after Mavis, saving our elderly dog from a weekend in kennels.

Tom knew Cecily was right but he is already missing her and half-composing messages that he will send when he has the chance. But now that he's sitting here, next to his dad and opposite his sisters, he sees that his girlfriend was right.

"I'll deal," he says, an unspoken agreement that the game will be American Whist. It always is. Kitty finds some paper and a pen in her bag. The refreshments trolley is trundled down the aisle by a cheerful moustachioed man, and Graham gets three cans of G&T, and an apple juice for Annie.

"Gin at this time of the morning, Dad?" Kitty pretends to be shocked.

"Well, we're celebrating, aren't we?" *Are we?* he wonders.

"Yes. We are," Kitty says firmly. She wants to say more but now is not the time or place. "And I'm really looking forward to having this weekend with all of you. Cheers."

"Cheers," they respond, and they raise their drinks towards the centre of the table, and take a sip before card-playing begins in earnest.

I can't help but smile as I watch them, and I'm beginning to feel less left out, less sore, that I can no longer participate. It's a healing time for all of us. Just seeing them enjoying being together is a balm for me. And I have to admit being back on this familiar train journey is a treat.

Watching not just my family but the other passengers too, and trying to keep up with the countryside and tiny stations that fly past the windows. It takes me back to those wonderful occasional weekends I would have when I'd escape for a day or two, down to London to meet up with my friend Justine, who had been a trainee nurse with me and who lives down in Brighton now with her partner Trudi and their five assorted dogs. We'd book a hotel, months in advance, and find tickets for a show. Choose a restaurant for dinner and spend the following day mooching down Oxford Street, just relishing some proper time with each other, and me savouring some grown-up, non-parent, non-wife, non-work time. I would think how life had been like that for a while before Graham, and I'd never appreciated it enough.

I loved the busyness of London. The mix of people;

the way nobody bats an eyelid at what somebody else is wearing; what colour hair (or skin) somebody has; what language they're speaking, or how they choose to present themselves to the world. I loved spending time with Justine and just sitting enjoying a coffee – sometimes followed by another; maybe a piece of cake, catching up on each other's lives, swapping news of other ex-students, discussing politics and the state of the world, safe in the knowledge we saw things from a similar vantage point.

The train journeys were an important part of the weekends away too; I would relish two full hours to sit and read, uninterrupted, and I'd keep my fingers crossed that I might not have to share my seat – and that if I did it wouldn't be with a talker. Not to be unsociable but because I cherished any chance to be quiet in those busy, child-ruled days. Time to myself was sacred.

Today, I would like nothing more than to join in with my family's card-playing, and to be caught up in the anticipation of the weekend; a nice hotel and a meal out. But it is not to be. I take myself away; two carriages along, to be precise, because I happen to know there is somebody else important on this train. Quite by chance, my lovely Nick is also heading to London this weekend. He is meeting his daughter, and her new partner. He is nervous. I see that in the way his left hand squeezes a napkin, while his right holds his book. In the way that he goes back to the same part of the page more than once, his eyes having been running across the words while his mind is actually jumping ahead to this planned meeting.

He and his daughter get on better than they used to but she is wary of him, believing him to be a man who left his family for his work. He has never told her or his son that in fact it was their mother having an affair that was the catalyst. But he knows that really, his behaviour was the catalyst for his ex-wife having an affair. He shoulders the blame admirably.

I think of how he and Annie and I have all protected people this way. Graham, Alex and Nick's wife – their misdemeanours shielded by our loyalty and wish to make life run smoothly. What does that say about us? We are altruistic angels, or just pushovers? Maybe it just means we are realists when it comes to human nature.

"Mind if I sit here?" I murmur, sliding into the empty space next to him. He doesn't move or react in any way and I'm disappointed though not surprised. It's selfish, to want them to notice me. I know that. And it may not be the comforting thing I imagine it to be. So I sit quietly, contentedly, and allow my mind to wander, to imagine if he and I were on a trip away together. I would have liked that, but would never have allowed it to happen. Nick had suggested it once but even as he'd let the words out of his mouth he knew it would not be. I just couldn't be that person. That cliché. And maybe if I am very honest, a little part of me wanted to feel superior to Graham, still smarting from his actions so many years before. I would not stoop to that level.

But I loved him – and I still do. Life is complicated. It's a little bit of a relief to be out of it, if I'm honest. Past all that. The human condition.

Nick turns the page of his book though he is getting nowhere with it. He sighs, closes his eyes. Despite his nerves, the motion of the train is making him sleepy and he allows himself to drift off, safe in the knowledge that London is the last stop. I lean against him as best I can and imagine for a while that things are different.

In time I head back along the train to my family. The card games are over for now. Graham too has opted to snooze and Kitty and Annie are reading, while Tom and Cecily are messaging back and forth.

I'm missing you already, he sends.

I miss you too. But you're going to have a great time.

I know, I know. I want to bring you to London one weekend.

That would be so good. I imagine the smile on Cecily's face at the thought of this. **How is Annie?**

She seems happy, unusually relaxed in fact.

Well that's got to be a good thing!

Yeah, I think so.

And Kitty?

She seems happy too. Dad's snoring though. In fact, I think he's dribbling... I might have to wake him.

Poor Graham! Leave him be. It doesn't matter, does it? And he can get some energy up for the weekend.

You are too kind.

I know.

The next stop is announced over the speaker system. Milton Keynes. Then it's home and dry to London. Graham does not react at all to the sounds of people getting on and off the train, but further along Nick has jolted awake, and is forced to smile and nod when a woman asks if the seat next to him is free.

She is about the same age as him, and I can see she thinks he's a nice-looking man. She's right. It takes a little bit of courage but she strikes up a conversation with him and I can tell he's not really keen on it, preferring the company of his own thoughts, but he is far too polite to ignore her. He smooths his napkin and places it carefully inside his book, marking his page, though he's going to have to go back a few pages anyway to follow the story. Then he turns to her and smiles.

Oh, that smile. I remember being lifted by it so many times, on the ward at work and then sometimes over post-work drinks, or dinner, or on a quiet walk in the countryside. I used to see how Nick could look so plain, and unassuming, and slip past people's attention. Even his clothes, and his haircut, are plain and unassuming. But if you caught him smiling like that at you, his eyes lit up and dancing with life, he looked like a different man, and once you'd seen that about him there was no way you could go back.

He listens now as the woman tells him she's meeting her sister to go shopping and to a show. And he finds himself telling her about meeting his daughter. He even admits he's a bit nervous, and is surprised to find himself opening up this little bit.

"It's difficult isn't it, when they're grown up? And you know how their partner might be judging you. And they might know things about you, that your kids tell them; family times when you might not have been at your best." I like this woman, I decide. And she has Nick's attention now. "God, there are times when they're little, and you're frazzled, and you might have shouted at them or something, just from pure exhaustion, and that moment's gone right into their little consciousnesses. Even if it's just one moment among a million where you've got the patience of a saint. That's the one that sticks. And then they grow up and they're like, *Mum used to shout at me when I was little*." She laughs.

"God, it's true," Nick says. "I mean, I left them when they were quite young, my two."

"Oh," she says but not unsympathetically. And Nick finds himself telling her about his marriage, and his wife having an affair, and him leaving shortly after he found out.

"But you never told your kids? About your wife cheating on you?"

"No," he admits. "Because I think – I thought, no I do still think – it was my fault really."

The woman is taken aback. "But that's – you're – so lovely. And ridiculously understanding!"

"I wasn't the best husband." His soft voice betrays his Scottish roots.

"Who is?" she laughs, but I see her shoot a glance of wonder at my lovely Nick and I know she sees what I saw in him. What I still see. He is such a good man.

"And so I know you're right; kids talk, tell their boyfriends and girlfriends about their past. And I'll have been cast as this work-driven, emotionless dad, who put his career before his family. It's true in some ways. I loved my work. So much I couldn't really retire when I tried to. I still love my work. It's who I am."

And then they're talking about his job at the hospital, and I know an image of me flits through his mind. His eyes glance up, in fact, and it's as if he's seen me. But I know he hasn't. He can't. And I also know that's really for the best.

I leave them to it and return again to my family, where Graham is back in the land of the living, and checking his wallet and his phone and his keys, making sure he still has everything he needs, even though having been hemmed in by Tom, and not having moved for the entire journey, there is really very little chance of having lost anything. As the train draws closer to Euston, people begin lifting their bags down from luggage racks, putting away their books or tablets, zipping up pockets and pulling on jackets because, though it's well into early summer now, it's not the warmest of days.

Annie feels her own jacket is a bit snugger than it would have been a few weeks ago, and she's actually excited by the thought. She runs her hand smoothly over her belly and Graham sees this, and smiles at her. His eldest daughter returns his smile, and he is warmed by it. She looks happy, he thinks. Almost relaxed. And for the first time since I died, though he doesn't necessarily realise this, a feeling of pure warmth and love floods through Graham, untouched by grief or anger or bewilderment. He is simply glad to be here with his children, with a lovely weekend ahead.

They wait their turn, joining the queue of other passengers shuffling slowly along the aisle and off the train. Graham turns to help Annie as she steps off and, although her internal reaction is 'I don't need any help', she lets him. It makes him happy.

They wait for Tom and Kitty to disembark as well, and then begin to make their way along the platform. Just as they are getting close to the ticket gates into the main concourse, my husband feels a hand on his shoulder and hears a voice behind him.

"It's Graham, isn't it? I thought it was you."

11

It's not Nick, although actually he has done a double-take on disembarking, recognising my family immediately. He stays well back, and shakes his head with a wry little smile. *Bloody hell Ruth,* he thinks, and I think, *I know.*

But no, it's not him tapping my husband on the shoulder – thank God, because that would be weird – it's actually Sandra, the woman who rescued Mavis and helped when Tom had his accident. She's been on the same train, in the same carriage, as my family, and nobody had noticed. Not even me.

Graham turns, taken aback, and it takes a moment for him to recognise her, but Kitty knows immediately who it is.

"Sandra!" she says and, well aware of Graham's tendency to forget people's names if he doesn't have to use them on a daily basis she says, "Dad, it's Sandra, who helped rescue…"

"I know who Sandra is, thank you!" Graham interrupts, just a tiny note of sharpness in his voice. We all – me included – look at him and he recovers himself, smiling at Kitty before shining that same smile on Sandra. "Hello, how are you? And what a coincidence, us all being in London."

As he says this, Nick walks past, scurrying round the other side of a pillar, thinking, *You don't know the half of it.*

"I know! I'm, well, shopping. With my daughter. This is Tasha."

A lovely looking young woman steps forward slightly, from her mother's side. "Hi," she says, although she clearly has no idea who anyone else is.

"Hi!" Kitty steps into the breach once more. "I'm Kitty. Your mum is our family hero."

"Oh?" Tasha laughs, clearly considering that Kitty might be a bit mad.

"This is the family I told you about," Sandra looks meaningfully at her daughter and Tom catches this, reddening. Does this mean she's told Tasha about him running off and knocking himself unconscious? Yes, of course she has, though she doesn't choose that detail to focus on now. "Mavis' family."

"Oh… Mavis! Oh, she's so lovely! I was at Mum's when she brought her back…"

Damn, now it's clear that she must know the story. But Tom smiles gamely. "She is lovely. Getting on a bit now. My girlfriend is with her."

"Oh that's nice. So you four can have a family weekend away?"

"Yes, it's–" Graham stops himself saying it's our

anniversary – "good to have a chance to get away."

"I'm sure," smiles Sandra. "And we're wedding dress shopping," she adds. All of my lot are too busy thinking about that dramatic weekend when they met her, to think to ask her about herself.

"You're getting married?" Graham asks, obtusely.

"Not me!" Sandra laughs. "Tasha."

"Oh, yes, of course." It's Graham's turn to flush now. "I mean, not 'of course', there's no reason you shouldn't be getting married…"

"Oh, there is. Every reason!" Sandra laughs good-naturedly.

"Fair enough!" he grins.

With unspoken agreement, the six of them begin heading towards the ticket gates once more.

"So that's exciting," Kitty says to Tasha.

"Yeah! I'm not all that bothered about dresses to be honest, I'm not being a bridezilla, but it's a nice chance to get away with Mum."

"I bet," Kitty says, pushing away the thought that she would so love to be able to do the same with me.

"Oh," Tasha remembers what Sandra told her, about the lovely, lost dog and her lovely, lost family. "I'm sorry. Mum told me, about…"

"It's OK," Kitty smiles. "It's great that you're making the most of having your mum. Mums are important!" Noticing Annie at her side, she squeezes her sister's hand briefly. "So are you down for the day, or staying over?"

"We've got a hotel, over near Hyde Park."

"We're staying that way as well!" Kitty says.

"Oh really? Well my fiancé's band is playing tonight, and I said I'd go and see them. We booked a hotel nearby, so I don't have far to go. It's not Mum's scene and she didn't want me traipsing the Streets of London late at night on my own. They're a great band. You guys should come!"

Tom, hearing this and being heavily into his music, begins asking questions. "Oh yeah, I think I might have heard of them," he says, aware that his sisters exchange a look. "I have!" he protests indignantly, immediately the little brother.

"You might have, if you listen to Radio 6 a lot," says Tasha.

"Yes!" Tom says. "I do." *See?* his look says to his sisters. "Where are they playing?"

Tasha gives him the details, as they join the narrowing funnel of people waiting to be allowed into London by the automated gates.

"Brill!" he says, and he turns to look for Graham, who is in deep conversation with Sandra. "Dad, we could go and see a band tonight!"

Graham looks at his son and laughs, seeing that childlike earnestness he's always had. "Maybe, son!" he looks at Sandra, who smiles, and once more Tom feels thwarted, belittled by his family. Why shouldn't his dad come and see a band, for God's sake? He wishes Cecily was with him.

Once they are through the gates, the group heads towards the Underground but Graham puts his hand on Kitty's shoulder. "I need the loo," he says quietly, like it's something to be ashamed of. He clearly doesn't want Sandra hearing. Because Sandra, of course, being a nurse will be entirely unaware of the necessity of bodily functions. Interesting that he cares what she thinks, though, and I can see Kitty is considering the same thing.

"Sandra!" she says, and the woman turns. "We're going to stop to use the facilities. It was lovely to see you, hopefully we can meet up for a dog walk sometime back home?"

"Lovely!" says Sandra. "Enjoy your family weekend." She addresses them all but she is looking at Graham. "It sounds like it's going to be very special."

"And you enjoy wedding dress shopping," Graham says slightly gruffly. "Lovely to meet you, Tasha."

"You too!" she beams. "Maybe see you later?" She looks to Annie, Kitty and Tom.

"Maybe," says Tom keenly.

"What was that about, kids? Seeing them later?" Graham asks as the four of them make an abrupt u-turn and head back to the queue for the toilets.

"I said, Dad," Tom says slightly exasperatedly. "There's a gig tonight. Her bloke's band's playing tonight, not far from where we're staying. I've heard them, they're pretty good."

"But we probably won't go," says Kitty, shooting a

look at Tom that says, *This is our family weekend. And we're not leaving Dad alone on his first anniversary without Mum.*

"Let's see, shall we?" an unusually relaxed Graham says, and Tom shoots a look back at his sister.

That's the way, Graham! I think, recognising this version of him better than his children do. For all his stressed ways at home, get Graham away on a weekend in a city, or for a week by the sea, and he eases into a different version of himself, the pressures of home and, previously, work, having been shed somewhere along the way. The children won't necessarily know this; our family holidays were not always the most relaxing, but I've come to wonder if anyone's really are. After the three of them grew older and stopped coming away with us though, Graham and I had some lovely trips together.

We came to London a number of times, and it was a revelation to have time to spend just relaxing; a drink in a riverside bar, watching the world go by and feeling no need to speak; an art exhibition without children complaining it was boring; a West End show, or a meal out at a nice restaurant. Though it was different to those heady days when we first got together and Graham seemed like my absolute world, coming out the other side of raising children had given us a new way to appreciate each other. And Graham, often taciturn at home, was sociable, interested in people we met, and in turn interesting too. I began to love him again in a different way, and sometimes felt conflicted when I considered what I also had with Nick.

As Graham goes to use the loo, Kitty, Tom and Annie stand together, amid the craziness of the station concourse. A great number of people are standing staring at the information board, putting me in mind of penguins. At the addition of platform information for the imminent departure to Liverpool Lime Street, a section split themselves away, hurrying towards their train.

"Thanks for waiting!" Graham says, putting his arm round Tom. He is swept up in the energy of the place, and Tom's irritation at his dad melts away. He puts a friendly arm around him in return and the four of them head off towards the Underground.

Annie takes charge here, well used to navigating the twists and turns of the city when she comes for work. Graham, too, is no stranger to London, though it's been a while and he's happy for Annie to be their guide. She stands back and watches them all go safely through the gates before following on, then it's down the escalators, forming part of the endless lines of people who are being transported down into the belly of the Earth, and on to the Northen Line platform. Kitty and Tom both feel slightly out of their comfort zones, though neither would want to admit it.

Annie shepherds them onto the train and tells them which stations they're going through till they have to get off then walk to the District Line, for Monument, and a short ride to Tower Hill.

When they reach their destination, they feel almost swallowed up by a sea of tourists, of so many different nationalities. Emerging from the station into a blue-skied day, they blink, getting their bearings.

"There's plenty of time," Annie says, "but shall we head towards the cruise now? We can always get a drink somewhere if we want to."

"Can I carry your bag, Annie?" Graham says, feeling he should be doing more to look after his pregnant daughter, but he already knows what her answer will be.

"No, I'm fine!" she says firmly. "I packed light anyway." And without another word, Annie begins to lead the way once more, her dad and her siblings following on obediently.

Annie is a bit tired but she is also buzzing. She has reached that golden part of her pregnancy that people talk of, and although it had felt like that sickness would never leave her, it's finally slunk away, tail between its legs, and she's not sure she's ever felt so alive. As she walks, she is picturing bringing her child to London one day; taking it to all the museums and art galleries, maybe a show. They could make it an annual thing, lasting all the way into her child's adulthood... It is not like Annie to think this way, and

I like it – and so does she. In her mind, it will be just her and the child. No more men. She won't have time for relationships anyway, if she's going to make it work going freelance. Because what Meg says has struck a chord and Annie is thinking more and more seriously about going it alone. But, Annie being Annie, she is not going to make any rash moves. She has a lot of research to do, and a lot of gentle sounding-out of clients. She knows she can't just steal them; that will land her in serious trouble, but if they might recommend her to others, and eventually find their own way to her, well what can she do?

So Annie is full of – everything. Energy, life, positivity and confidence.

Graham is relaxed, trying to think of our anniversary with gratitude for having had me in his life, and for having his children around to help carry him through this difficult weekend.

Tom is excited, by the city and by the thought of a potential night out, if he can swing it.

And Kitty is drinking in the sights and sounds of the city, ideas whizzing at her like tube trains. She needs to find some time to make some notes and sketches if she can.

The four of them head towards the Tower Millennium Pier, where their lunch cruise awaits them. I know I'm in each of their minds but there is so much else going on, and I stupidly, tearfully, feel a little bit left behind.

"I know this sounds stupid," Kitty says to Tom as they walk, "but it feels like we're leaving Mum behind."

My beautiful girl. How does she know?

"It doesn't sound stupid. I feel it, too. Every day is a step further away from the last one when she was alive."

My boy, too, and then...

"She'd have loved this," says Annie. Graham is distracted, gazing up at the buildings they pass by. Annie too had been admiring the incredible designs, but she heard her brother and sister putting into words what she was feeling. Spontaneously, my three children squeeze each other's hands and that act sends a whoosh of warmth into me, like a hot tap has been turned on. They look at each other and laugh, shrugging their shoulders. Did they feel it too?

"Come on Dad," Tom says kindly, putting his hand on Graham's shoulder. "There'll be time for architecture-gazing later. For now, our boat awaits."

They had told Graham they were having a cruise on the Thames but the lunch is a surprise. He laughs when he realises and when they are seated he looks around at each of them, as if seeing them with fresh eyes.

"I do not know what I'd do without you three," he says.

He says this a lot but today they are feeling just a little bit more emotional and around the table, eyes are glistening.

"Tell us about your wedding, Dad," encourages Kitty.

"Well... what, really?"

She nods and Tom does too. "Yes, go on, Dad," says Annie, though she herself is feeling bruised and more than a little cynical about the whole marriage thing at the moment.

"Well, it was a beautiful day. Not weather-wise. It was pissing it down."

That makes them all laugh.

"But I remember I could hardly sleep the night before and thankfully Peter was there, meant to be sleeping on a mattress on the floor of my room, but I made him get up and go for a walk with me, at some ungodly hour of the morning."

"I can't imagine Peter was too happy about that." Tom chuckles, thinking of Graham's lifelong friend, now a large and somewhat immovable mountain of a man.

"Ah, he used to love all that stuff. Camping, fishing, hiking... anyway, that's by the by. When we got up for that walk, it was already raining but it was warm. It had already been light for hours and I remember stepping out, thinking what a magical day it was going to be and what a magical date..." He stops, and swallows. I am spellbound. I have heard this story before, of course, but never told with such feeling. "I remember feeling so excited about seeing your mum, but so nervous too. What if she didn't turn up? Or changed her mind? Or some other suitor spoke up, during the ceremony? Or her dad expressed his dissatisfaction with the match…"

This makes them laugh. My dad absolutely loved Graham. My mum, too. I could never have told them about his affair, it would have broken their hearts. But today is not a day for thinking about that. I remember it too, that rainy late spring day. Of course, I do. I do.

It was warm, and I too had not been able to sleep. I was at my parents' house and my sister was there, and all of us rose and ended up downstairs at an ungodly hour of the morning, as if by some unspoken invitation. Mum put the kettle on and Dad cooked bacon sandwiches, though I remember being too nervous to really feel like eating. "Go on Ruth," he'd encouraged. "It will build you up for the day."

So I ate, in small mouthfuls, tasting the melted butter and feeling the soft white bread sticking to the roof of my mouth. It felt quite momentous for us as a family; our little house of four was about to be broken into; a bit snapped off and shared with somebody else. My sister, I remember, was quiet, and I think she was worried about what me getting married would mean for us and our close relationship. We had loved each other all our lives and rarely argued.

Mum was feeling it too, and Dad, though he tried to

be jovial and jokey and keep the atmosphere lifted. Outside, the rain poured down, running down the windows and pooling on the pavers.

"It'll lift later," Dad tried to reassure me. "It's just getting it all out of the way now."

He was wrong. It rained all the way through to early evening, but it didn't matter.

I tune back into Graham's story-telling. "When I arrived at the church there were already a few of our friends and relatives gathered outside, so I had to step up and try and hide my nerves and excitement. It was a lot of small talk, and introducing people to each other, all sheltered underneath the little porch until the vicar opened up and we were able to go inside. And gradually, the church filled up, and Peter was great, showing people where to sit and then coming back and trying to keep me cool, calm and collected."

"We should have brought some pictures," Kitty says.

"I've got this one." Graham pulls out his wallet and slides a battered and creased photograph from it, which shows me and him in the middle, our parents either side of us. It makes me smile, and transports me back to that exact moment. Peter had taken that photo, in fact, and I remember standing there, holding Graham's hand tightly, and just before Peter had shouted, "Say cheese!" Graham had said, "I love you, Mrs Hebden," and leaned forward to kiss me, and I'd thought I could never have imagined feeling so happy.

They pass the photo round, though they've all seen

it before of course. But they take their time, looking at me, as if trying to see something, trying to find me, and then looking more closely at their grandparents, who would have only been in their fifties but somehow still managed to look aged even then.

Graham smiles at the image of me as he slides the picture back into its place, and says, "She was late, you know. To the wedding."

They do know; they've heard this before, but each of them want to let Graham tell his story. Our kind children.

"I thought she'd changed her mind, that she wasn't going to come. My god, my hands were sweaty, and I started to think of how I'd let people know. How to break the news that they had wasted their Saturday, some of them travelling from miles away, and that – that she didn't love me after all."

Graham's voice breaks here. Kitty, sitting next to him, puts her hand on his shoulder. "But she did, Dad. She did love you, and she did marry you."

But he's gone. The memory has proved too much for him and Graham is broken, suddenly, sobbing as he thinks of that day, and all the days since; all that he had, and all that he has lost.

Kitty slides her hand across to his other shoulder, and lets him lean on her, sobbing it out while Annie and Tom sit awkwardly across from them and some of the other passengers try not to look.

It doesn't take too long for the tears to subside but the moment is gone, and now the boat is full and the barrier's been closed. The tour guide is making some safety announcements and a waiter comes to check food orders. It is a limited menu – one meat dish (roasted supreme of chicken) and one veggie (oyster mushroom and white bean cassoulet) but it's not about the food.

Annie has ordered a bottle of champagne, unbeknown to the others, and as the boat moves away from its mooring, the tour guide already in full, cheeky swing with his well-practised patter, the waiter brings it over, and pops it open, smoothly pouring and handing out the frothing glasses. The nosier of their fellow diners wonder what the deal is with my family, where the older man had been crying his eyes out not long before yet they seem to be celebrating something. It's easy to put two and two together, though, and this provokes some sympathetic glances, and some hand-squeezing of partners as people consider their luck, and the older ones contemplate what life may have in store for them.

"To Mum and Dad," Annie says, leading the toast and even allowing herself a small drink of champagne.

"To Mum and Dad," echo Tom and Kitty.

"To Ruth," says Graham. "The love of my life."

Seated near the side of the boat, they are able to look out towards the Tower of London, and let the tour guide's voice and chuckles of their fellow passengers lift them. And soon they are laughing too, and listening to the guide's stories, of some of the past residents of the Tower, and how the Vikings once destroyed London Bridge, and of course the Great Fire of London. As the boat moves along the river, my family find their minds and their moods are moving too, easing away from the quiet sadness and grief; even Graham is relaxing, the champagne bubbles elevating his enjoyment. When the food comes, he finds he is able to tuck in with gusto and he listens, laughing, to Tom's tale of a stag do he'd been on in London.

By the time they've returned to dock, the four of them are in high spirits, and as they leave the boat Graham pushes a tenner into the tour guide's tip bucket, saying, "That was fantastic, thank you."

"Thank you, sir. Glad you enjoyed it."

And all of a sudden, they are back in the real world, a little tipsy and slightly misty-eyed, but having to navigate their way amongst throngs of tourists and across busy roads.

"Let's go and find somewhere to sit," Kitty suggests.

"I know just the place," says Graham and somehow he is Dad again, confidently leading his little group of children like three chicks following Mother Hen along a busy, bustling pavement.

"Coffee!" he pronounces grandly, and the three of them look at each other, chuckling.

There is of course, nowhere that is not busy in central London, but when they reach the Tower

Bridge Piazza they manage to find a bench that is just being vacated and Graham sits his children down. "Stay put!" he says, and after about fifteen minutes he returns with a tray of takeaway cups. "This one is decaf," he says to Annie, and then he hands cups to Kitty and Tom too. Kitty moves off the bench to make space for Graham, ignoring his protests, and sits on the grass next to it.

"This is great," she says, her eyes scanning the view and the passersby. "What a lovely day!"

"You look just like your mum," Graham says, and it makes Kitty swallow. "I remember her face, when we left the reception. Weddings weren't like they are now, and we were heading to London that night. We stepped outside, and the rain had stopped, and there was that smell —"

"Petrichor," says Tom.

"That's right. I always think that sounds wrong, like something chemical, but I remember it that day; the freshness after the rain, and your mum said something about it being symbolic, of our lives with each other just beginning…"

Oh, I did. I fancied myself as a real romantic back then. But I meant it too. I was so sincere and so in love.

"I can imagine that," says Kitty.

"And we only had three days away, down here in London, but they were magical. I don't think I've ever been so happy. Well apart from when you three were born," he adds.

119

"You don't have to say that, Dad!" Tom protests. "I can imagine just how it felt." And, thinking of Cecily, he really can.

Oh, to be that age again, where your relationship seems like the answer to everything, passionate and untainted by the inevitable trials and challenges, and heartbreaks, of life as it progresses, as it must.

Kitty and Annie look at each other.

"I saw that!" Tom says. "Don't patronise me."

"We're not, Tom, really," Kitty says. "Honestly, it's lovely. You and Cecily are lovely, together."

Tom smiles slightly, still not entirely sure that his big sisters aren't having him on. "Yeah, well…"

"Really, Tom," says Annie, laying her hand on his shoulder, and the fact that it's Annie convinces him.

And they sit for a while, sipping their coffees, each lost in their own private thoughts.

12

"Are you alright, Dad?" Kitty sees Graham rubbing his eyes.

"What? Oh, yes, thanks love. Just a bit tired."

"Well it's getting on now you know, I bet we could check into the hotel, you could have a power nap."

"I could do with one of them," Annie says, surprising the others. It's not like her to admit to needing any kind of rest, perhaps seeing it as a kind of weakness – she would deny the need to ever sleep or eat if she could.

"Let's go then, shall we? If that's OK with you, Dad?"

"Oh, yes, I'm happy to go along with what everybody thinks is best."

"We could all just chill for a bit before dinner."

They have chosen a hotel based on their restaurant booking, at a lovely family-run Italian place not far from Hyde Park. It is a place Graham and I have eaten at many times over the years, the first time being on our honeymoon. It's difficult to know whether it is wise for Graham to be revisiting these places, especially so soon, but he'd thought long and hard about it, and talked it through with Kitty. The little hotel we stayed at has been swallowed up into an apartment block, which I don't think is a bad thing, and so the four of them have booked into a nice old converted townhouse. I say townhouse but it's enormous. Their footsteps ring on the polished marble floor as they go across to the reception desk. Graham takes charge here, giving his name and card details, and each of them is handed a key card.

"Meet back here at six?" Graham asks.

"Perfect." Somehow it is already after four pm.

My husband and children head off in search of their rooms. Kitty is gratified to find hers is at the top of the hotel and the windows look out over the neighbouring rooftops, just allowing a peep at Hyde Park.

Annie's is on the ground floor, Tom's tucked somewhere on the first, and Graham's is down in the basement, with very little natural light. He does not care. He flops gratefully onto the bed and is off to sleep within minutes.

Tom, meanwhile, is of course on the phone to Cecily. "How is everyone?" she asks.

"Yeah – good, I think. Even Annie seems to have relaxed."

"And is Graham OK?"

"Yes, I think so. I think he might be glad to be away from home. There are plenty of distractions to keep him busy. He does look tired, though. How are you? How's Mavis?"

"We're good! We've been at the barrow this morning, just chilling out up there."

"She walked to the barrow?" Tom knows how old age is catching up with our beloved dog.

"No, I drove, we took the car and just walked up the path to it. That seemed to be enough for her. We sat on one of the benches, and saw Val and Derek. They sent their best wishes."

"Ah that's nice. I do like those two."

"Yeah, they're great!"

"You're pretty great yourself." Tom smiles and I suddenly feel guilty about listening in on their conversation. Boundaries are a strange thing when you're not alive in the world anymore. I can't pretend I'm not endlessly interested in my children's lives, and these days I have access to a lot more knowledge of them than I've ever had before. I do have to stop sometimes and think, would they want me to know this? Then again, what possible harm can it do? But no, I must still respect their privacy. Some of the time, at least.

Annie is lying on her bed, listening to a meditation on the Headspace app. Since her night at Kitty's, Meg has kept in touch with her and she's got Annie into the idea of using this app to help her get back to sleep when she's having a bad night, and just to take time out during the day. She hasn't let on to anyone about any of this, and Meg has not shared with Kitty anything of the conversations they've had, but as well as preparing for motherhood, Annie's mind is now also running almost constantly through the idea of going it alone with work. She's been reading up about it, talking to HMRC, looking at other similar businesses – often, but not always, run by other women. Ryan Edwards still has two months to go of his leave period at his current place of work so he's not been in the office much yet but he has sent her emails asking for information and background on clients, etc. Annie has to take a deep breath – and often utilises the Headspace app in this instance too – before reacting or replying. She is cool, calm, measured, and not letting on about anything, to anyone. But, as the cliché about the swan goes, all is calm on the surface while below the water those beautiful webbed feet are doing a lot of work. I watch her now, as she listens to the soothing voice instructing her to imagine a ray of sunshine filling and warming her whole body, beginning with her feet. It makes me smile.

In Kitty's room, her portrait of me is sitting in front of the mirror and my middle child is on the bed, in floods of tears. *It's alright*, I tell her, lying down beside her. I know she's alright with crying. She thinks it's healthy. She's not wrong. For Kitty allows herself these times when the pent-up emotions can come out, and she always feels better for them. But today she is feeling sorry for herself as well. There is something about Tom and Cecily's relationship that she's struggling with, just a bit. She is happy for her brother, of course. And she loves Cecily. But, she wonders, will she ever find anyone? She is still angry with herself over what happened with Alex. And embarrassed. There is an element of self-pity; she knows her dad is broken now but he's had a lifetime of love and to her and the others, the relationship that we had was close to perfect. They don't, of course, know about his secretary and nor do they know about Nick. She suspects that Annie, while separated from Alex, could probably have her husband back any time she wants, Donna or no Donna. But even if that wasn't the case, Annie has the baby. What if Kitty never get the chance to be a mum? She feels an intense tap of anxiety on her chest, though she is so young. She has plenty of time, but who ever believes that when they're in the grip of loneliness? Kitty's last relationship was with the obnoxious and self-centred Ollie. Neither Graham nor I ever liked him.

"I'm just lonely," she says now, letting her tears speak volumes. "So lonely. Oh Mum." And this is what I mean about boundaries. Kitty is allowing herself to wallow in this moment but it's because she is alone. She has turned on the tap of sorrow to control when, where and how it comes out. I run my hand across her hair and leave her be.

Graham is snoring on his bed. I had thought he might be struggling more than he is, but looking at him now I see he's doing alright. I lie down next to him and rest as well, listening to the sounds of other guests in the hotel and from the street outside. This city is so busy and restless.

Graham snores a little and wriggles around, finding his favoured comfortable position on his side. I curl myself around him, hoping he feels it somehow. My love and my warmth, for this man I shared most of my life with. For better or worse. Mostly for better. Lucky me.

At half past six, Kitty, now showered and changed and looking fresh as a daisy, is knocking on Graham's door. The phone calls have failed to wake him. "What? MMmff…" He is confused at first, and feels a trail of saliva running down his chin and pooling on his pillow.

"Dad," Kitty says gently. "Are you awake?"

He sits up, pushing his fingers through his hair, feeling his heart beat too fast. "Just coming."

Off the bed and across the floor to the door, opening it. "Hello love."

"Were you still asleep?" Kitty asks sympathetically. "Sorry, Dad, it's just our table's booked for seven-thirty. I thought you might want to freshen up first."

"I think that would be good."

"No worries, no rush. We'll be in the hotel bar. Take your time and come down to meet us when you're ready, then we can walk to the restaurant. It's only a few minutes away."

"Alright love." Graham is doing his best to appear

together and in control. "I'll just hop in the shower and then I'll be down."

"Hopping in the shower sounds a bit dangerous, Dad," Kitty grins.

"Oh yes, very good." He smiles. Reaches out and strokes her hair. "Thanks love."

"What for?"

"For looking out for me."

"Any time, Dad." She steps forward and hugs him briefly. "See you downstairs."

In the bar, Annie and Tom are chatting. It's rare that it's just the two of them but Annie has found herself telling him about her work. She hadn't intended to but finds that her thoughts are bubbling out of her.

"Listen to this, Kitty! Annie's going it alone, with work."

Kitty diplomatically looks surprised, not wanting Tom to know that she is already privy to this information.

"Well, no, well yes, well not definitely..." This floundering is far from typical of Annie.

"You must!" Kitty says. "Annie, you're so talented and smart, and I just – I don't think that you should be working for anyone else. If anything I think they should be working for you."

This expression of admiration takes Annie by surprise and she smiles at her sister. "Really?"

"Yes! And now this baby's coming... and you're

independent. It's a chance to look at things differently, isn't it? Do things differently. I know it's not as straightforward as that. I know you need an income... But you know, if you needed help, Dad would be there like a shot. He's helped me out, you know."

Her brother and sister politely pretend they didn't know this.

"And I'm bloody living at home again!" Tom says ruefully. "So he's putting an actual roof over my head."

"Bet he pays for all the food too, doesn't he?" Kitty grins.

"He – well, I do the shopping," Tom tries to put up a protest.

"It's OK, Tom. It doesn't matter, does it? What's important right now is that we're all together and all looking out for each other, in whatever way is necessary. I'm not too proud to say I don't have a lot of money," says Kitty. "But I work bloody hard and I'm hoping that I can get myself into a better position one of these days."

"Keep going," Annie says, "with what you love. Honestly, Kitty, I couldn't imagine you doing anything differently."

"We're lucky," Tom acknowledges, "really lucky, to have parents... a dad... who can help us out."

"And who wants to," agrees Kitty.

"But wouldn't we all do the same if we could?"

"Yes," Annie agrees, her hand on her belly and her mind on her future. "We would, and we will, all support each other in every way that we can. That is what Mum would want us to do."

"I feel bad leaving Dad," Kitty says.

"Honestly, I don't think he minded, at all." Tom is enlivened by the idea of a night out, still young enough to have a second and maybe even third wind, even after their long day of travelling, sight-seeing and difficult emotions.

"He's really tired," agrees Annie, her brother and sister trying not to look at her in wonder. I too am slightly in awe of this new version of my daughter; but I see it too, her internal turmoil and her determination to do the best by her baby but also by herself. Her initial reaction to Tom's suggestion that they come out and see the band Tasha mentioned was to say no, but she stopped herself and agreed immediately.

Tom had been shocked; he'd really thought it would be just him and Kitty, which is a familiar dynamic. They've had some unforgettable nights out together, dating back to their late teenage years, and they make a good team, matched in energy and in temperament. In fact, a small part of him thought, oh no, when Annie agreed, as he imagined his slightly socially awkward older sister sitting straight-faced and disapproving, sipping a soda water.

"Great!" he'd said, though, and now, flanked by his

older sisters, he's glad she's come. Especially as she seems unusually relaxed and high-spirited.

"I'm impressed, Annie," he says as they peer at doorways, trying to find the right place.

"By what?"

"You. I thought you might just want to stay at the hotel too. It must be tiring for you, being...?"

"Pregnant?" Annie says. "I suppose it is, in a way, but right now I feel more full of life than I have in a long time. I mean, I am literally full of life–" she gestures to her belly – "but that horrible sickness has been replaced by some real energy. It is so strange."

"And brilliant!" Kitty moves round behind Tom and squeezes in, linking arms with her brother and her sister. "And look at us all now, on a night out in London. Mum would be proud."

She hadn't meant to mention me and she immediately wishes she hadn't, not wanting to bring the mood down. But she is right; I am proud, and they are doing exactly what I asked them to do: living their lives. I would – and I do – only want them to make the most of their time and seeing them together like this is, unbeknown to them, the best wedding anniversary gift I could hope for.

These three are the real success of my relationship with Graham, love him though I do. It was never the same after his affair and my view of life and love changed dramatically but never faltered when it came to my children.

"That was such a lovely picture of her, Kit," Tom says.

"Do you think? Did Dad like it, do you think?" She has been fretting a bit about this.

"He loved it," her brother reassures her. He's not wrong. Right now, Graham is lying on his hotel bed, eating a bag of pistachio nuts, taking an occasional sip of red wine, and looking past his socked feet towards the dressing table mirror, where he has propped Kitty's picture of me. "Happy anniversary, Ruth," he murmurs, lifting his glass, and feeling his eyes fill with tears. The tears had come when Kitty gave him the portrait too, but they were the product of shock, surprise and pride, and love, for all of his children. Our children.

"Is this the place?" Annie asks, peering at a doorway next to one of those little kiosks that sell cigarettes and tobacco, papers, magazines, cold cans of pop, and postcards.

"Let's see," Tom says, pushing slightly past her. "Yeah, I think it is. Excuse me," he says to the doorman politely, "is this the Rhumbar?" At the same time seeing the name on the doorway.

The man laughs. "Looks like it."

"Great, thanks mate." Tom stands back for his sisters to go in, and they head down some stairs to a surprisingly large space with a stage set up for a band, a DJ booth, a bar, and not many unoccupied tables.

"Hey!" They hear a voice and recognise Tasha from earlier. "You came!"

"Hi," Kitty says, raising her voice to be heard above the booming bass. She can feel it travelling through her, from her feet all the way up to her temples. It feels good. "Yeah, we weren't ready for bed yet so we thought we'd come down. It's only about five minutes from our hotel."

"Perfect. Where are you staying?"

"Bennetts."

"No way! That's where we are! I felt bad leaving Mum but she said she was happy to stay in and watch some TV."

"Yeah we were just saying we felt bad leaving Dad too. It's his first wedding anniversary without Mum."

"Oh I'm sorry. That must be tough for all of you." Tasha sends a sympathetic smile around all of my children, though Tom and Annie can't hear what's being said. "Look, come and join me and my friends, if you'd like to?"

"Thanks," Kitty says, wondering if Annie will be OK with this. "That would be great."

She ushers her brother and sister towards Tasha's table, where a couple of young men move up, and an older man pulls back a chair, smiling at Annie. Kitty watches her sister, ready to intervene as she sometimes has to, to smooth things over, but she's pleased to see Annie just smiles and graciously accepts the offer.

"Martin," the man offers his hand to Annie.

"Anne," she says. "Or Annie."

"Nice to meet you, Anne." He smiles. "Are you a friend of Tasha's?"

"No, we only met today!" she laughs, liking his open, friendly face. "Her mum rescued our dog once. It's a long story." And one that she realises Tom may not want sharing with strangers.

"Sounds like it. What kind of dog is it?"

"A spaniel. She was my mum's, really."

"Was?"

"Yes. Mum died, last autumn."

"That's rough. I lost my dad a couple of years back."

"Really?"

"Yeah. And my mum died when I was a kid. So I'm an orphan. Like Oliver Twist." He grins, and it makes Annie smile.

"You don't look much like a scrawny street urchin." Her eyes scan his muscular arms.

"It's all the gruel," he says and she laughs.

Kitty, talking to Tasha still but keeping half an eye on her sister, relaxes, seeing Annie look surprisingly at ease. Sometimes she feels like she needs to – not baby-sit exactly, but keep an eye out for her older sister in social situations – but whoever that tall, dark and handsome stranger is sitting next to Annie, he seems to have hit a good note.

"Drink?" Tom asks.

"Yes please, can I have a rum and coke?"

"They do fancy cocktails too," Tasha says, "though you might have to get a second mortgage."

"Ah no, I'm good with something simple," Kitty says.

"Suits her personality," Tom grins, dodging a swipe from his sister's hand. "Tasha, would you like something?"

"No I'm fine thanks."

"I don't want to interrupt Annie, she looks otherwise engaged!" Tom says.

"Ah, that's Martin. He's a lovely guy."

"He looks it," says Kitty, smiling.

"Stop it, you perv," says Tom. "I'll get Annie a water."

"That's a bit mean!" laughs Tasha.

"No, she'll be happy with that. She's with child," Tom says, miming a round belly.

"You idiot, Tom!" Kitty is glad that Annie didn't see, though she can't help laughing at her brother.

"Is she? How exciting!" says Tasha. "It's all going on, then."

"Yeah, I guess it is."

As Tom heads to the bar, one of the stage crew appears, to test out the equipment. He gets a huge cheer, as though he's one of the band. Ten minutes later, it becomes apparent that he actually is one of the band.

"They're not that big yet!" Tasha shouts into Kitty's ear. "But they will be." She grins as the bassist waves subtly to her and Kitty smiles, thinking how nice that must feel. She looks at Annie, who is still being chatted up by Martin. How come her newly separated, pregnant sister is having more luck than she is? She knows it's daft but a small part of her can't help but feel it's Karma, for what happened with Alex.

"They're really good!" Tom raises his voice and his glass. "Cheers." He knocks his drink against Kitty's and Tasha's.

"I'm going to have to get up and dance," Tasha says, seeing a couple of her friends doing the same. "Want to come?"

They make their way onto the small dance floor and it's not long before it's packed.

"Do you dance?" Martin asks Annie.

"I do, but I'm…"

"Pregnant?" he asks, his eyes twinkling.

"Is it obvious?" she asks, casting a glance at her waistline. There is a visible bump to those of us who know her but to the unacquainted it could easily be overlooked.

"No, I just saw your brother doing this—" he mimics Tom's 'round belly' gesture.

"Oh my god, typical Tom!" Annie says, but she finds she's smiling. And it's good that this man already knows the situation. There won't be any misunderstanding.

"So does being pregnant mean you can't dance?"

"Erm. I don't suppose…"

He takes her hand and pulls her gently to her feet. In truth, Annie isn't much of a dancer but she stands good-naturedly and Martin leads her to a space at the edge of the dancefloor, and gently squeezes her hand before letting go of it and beginning to move. He is really tall, Annie realises, and she feels small next to him as he smiles down at her. She is smiling too; feeling wonderful, in fact. And it isn't long before their hands are joined again. Every now and then Martin checks in with her to make sure she's OK but she is in fact having the time of her life. And when the music becomes deeper; the singer's voice throatier, and the mood in the club somehow more intense, Martin pulls Annie to him gently, moving with her so that she feels incredibly sexy and womanly, knowing her baby is acknowledged and safe, but this beautiful, well-built man (who smells so good) has his hands on her waist and is looking at her, making her feel something she has never felt before.

Lust.

The word springs into her mind unbidden. Is that right? Is that what this is?

She looks into his dark eyes and sees the smile there, the kindness, but something more. Nothing can happen, she knows that, but…

"Just relax. Enjoy yourself," Martin says.

She just swallows, and smiles back. Closes her eyes and feels the beat of the music, the strength of the man. Keeps moving.

This dalliance has not gone unnoticed by Kitty and Tom, who cast occasional glances the way of their older sister, firstly to make sure she's OK and secondly to make sure they are not imagining things.

Looking at each other, shrugging and grinning, they turn their attention back to the band and become a part of Tasha's group, jumping, shouting and dancing to egg the musicians on.

By the end of the night everyone is hot, sweaty and tired, and more than ready for their beds.

"It's been lovely meeting you, Anne," says Martin. "Would it be OK to ask for your number?"

"You can ask," Annie says, finding a natural flirt within her that she'd had no idea was there.

"Please may I have your number?"

"Yes." She takes his phone from him, then has to give it back so he can unlock it, but she puts her number in and smiles.

"That is the right number, is it?"

"Of course!"

"I'll be in touch." He kisses her gently on the lips and she feels herself light up, though she tries not to show it.

Tasha has hugs for the three of them. "Let's catch up next time I'm back home, shall we?"

"That would be brilliant!" Tom says. He is feeling jubilant and happy to have unexpectedly seen a great new band play live.

Only Kitty is a bit subdued.

"Are you alright, sis?" Tom asks, nudging her as they walk back to the hotel.

"What? Oh yeah, just a bit tired, that's all."

"It's been a long day," he acknowledges. "But how about you, Annie? How was your night?"

"It was good thank you," she says primly but even Annie can't prevent herself from smiling.

Kitty laughs, despite herself. "That's one way of putting it! You look really happy, Annie."

My oldest child just smiles. And they get back to the hotel, heading into the lobby and saying goodnight and hugging each other before they head their separate ways once more.

13

Next up in this long year of 'firsts' is my birthday. A tough day, for everyone, although if I'm being picky this is a day which didn't always mean much to them when I was alive. There were countless birthdays I was left fuming when Graham apparently gave it nothing more than a cursory thought and acknowledgement. Presents and card – tick. A lie-in? A meal out? Even a meal cooked for me? These things would have been better than a box of chocolates, a bottle of perfume, or even the book that I really wanted; after all, those were all things I could have provided myself, had I really wanted to. But an acknowledgement that I might need – maybe even deserve – a bit of a rest, even just on one day of the year – well, that could have been priceless.

But it did not happen while the children were growing up. Even when Graham was getting more stuck in, back when I was ill, it was an unspoken acknowledgement that as soon as I began to recover, we'd get back to 'normal'. I believe his willingness to 'help' me (as though all those household chores and children's swimming lessons, parties, etc, were my responsibility and he was doing me a favour) was in part driven by genuine care for me and the other part guilt at his affair. And as time wore on, and he realised he wasn't going to get 'caught', and the space between him and that period of his life grew larger, I think he actually began to make peace with what he had done, maybe even play it down in his mind. He had been at fault, of course, but you know, it was a difficult time, and lots of men do it, don't they? Even women, sometimes.

I know I'm sounding cynical, but I know Graham. I know this is how he would have made it possible to live with himself, and with me.

Only when I became ill again last year did his guilt resurface, and all the more so when I died, mixed up in that murky, ugly swell of sorrow and remorse, grief and doubt, tumbling him around until he didn't know which way was up, although he'd occasionally resurface, gasping for air, before being dragged back down to the bottom once more.

Cynical, yes, but don't mistake that for me not caring – or not even understanding. I may sound like I am being hard on Graham when I talk about that affair he had, but I do think I'm allowed to. It was a kick in the guts for me at such a difficult time in my life. But I worked my way through it, and I came out the other side never letting on that I knew, and no longer hating him either. I read accounts of other relationships ruined by affairs; vengeful wives cutting up suits and ties, or going out to find somebody to cheat with themselves.

In honesty I came to look on it all with a slight superiority. That even the term 'cheating' was just a bit small-minded. That seeing somebody else – sleeping with somebody else – was not the worst thing in the world. The sneaking around and lying is worse. Lust is one thing (as Annie has recently discovered) but the underhand nature of an affair is hard to swallow. Hurried, whispered phone calls; clandestine meetings. Lies upon lies upon lies.

I didn't want to go down that route with Nick, but I also could not get him out of my head; couldn't let him out of my life. And we worked together – though I know that is a poor excuse. I could have left work, been transferred to another ward. I was weak, but I was also strong. I occasionally found myself trying to justify what I had with Nick by remembering what Graham had done all those years before, but I did not want to be that person. It's not an eye for an eye, in my book. I didn't want to be petty. But I did want to be with Nick.

And here he comes now; bright and early to wish me a happy birthday. I knew he was planning to and I meet him at his car as he gets out and looks around, taking in the bright morning light. He opens the boot, pulls off his shoes and pulls on his walking boots, though the ground is dry. Summer has come early this year and shows no signs of easing up.

He pulls a small rucksack onto his back, places his shoes neatly in the boot and shuts the lid, turning and looking towards the barrow, and sighing. His shoulders are down and I know he's finding this hard. Every day since I had my diagnosis has been a challenge. He has not been sanctioned to be involved in any of it: my illness, my care, my death, my funeral. His role is unofficial and hidden. His grief a dirty secret.

Yet to me it is beautiful; his love for me always was. He listened to me. He looked at me. And yes, I know, what we had was unmarred by the daily grind of family life. Once upon a time, I think Graham had not been able to get me out of his mind – and I know that was how I felt about him – so it's unfair to compare the two relationships. In truth, I did not want to be without either of them, greedy though that may be.

Nick takes a deep breath and goes to the roadside, waiting for a passing lorry and its car chaser before he crosses to the field entrance. As soon as he sets foot on the path, a pair of butterflies rise up from the long grasses, greeting him. He sees them and watches their progress across the field and into the blue. Then he begins to walk.

It's like a pilgrimage, he thinks, coming up here. He's not sure what he thinks of it all, and he's not sure what he should feel. Maybe something more than he does. He closes his eyes as he walks, and tries to feel me. But it's not as simple as that. I wish he knew I was here, with him, but there is a reason that he doesn't. I've come to realise I don't have to try so hard to make them feel my presence. That in itself is not so important. What matters is that they can live on without me.

Trudge, trudge, trudge. His feet find a rhythm and he sticks with it, eyes focused on the ground in front of him. He is turning something over in his mind, and that is the possibility of a phone call with the woman he met on the train to London.

Before she got off the train she had turned to him. "This is really out of my comfort zone but what do you think about us swapping numbers?'

"I... sure," Nick had said, "I'd like that."

"Really?" Her smile had livened up her face and Nick had experienced a glimpse of the younger her. "Names, too?"

"Wh- Oh, of course!" She had smiled again. "I'm Claire."

"Nick," he'd smiled back, and pulled a pen and a notebook from his bag, scribbling his number and neatly pulling the page out of the book. He passed it to Claire, and she tore it in half, less neatly, then wrote her name in nice, cursive letters that Nick immediately approved of, and put her number underneath. She laughed.

"What?" Nick asked.

"My daughter would be telling me I should have

just put your number straight into my phone!"

"Oh my god, you're right. I know that, too. But there's something nice, isn't there, about swapping numbers like this? I will put yours into my phone, but it's not the same as having your beautiful writing tucked away in my pocket."

Claire had blushed at this but laughed gamely. "No, that's right. It's more —" She stopped herself. She had been going to say it was romantic.

"It is," he'd agreed with the unspoken word. "It was lovely to meet you, Claire. I will be in touch."

And they had both left the train a little lighter on their feet than when they'd boarded it.

Now, Nick walks towards the long barrow and thinks he will call Claire later. They have spoken a few times already and each time the call has lasted over an hour. There is much to talk about and much they have in common, and both appreciate the break in their otherwise long, quiet evenings that somehow stretch out far longer than the whole day that has come before them.

And Nick can't even quite remember what she looks like, though he does recall a lovely smile. She is a widow, he has discovered, of more than ten years. She was young when her husband died and she misses him still but it feels like her life now is a different one to back then; like it's been split in two. Nick worries that she will think him awful if he reveals his relationship with me. But today, he thinks, he might tell her. Because today I am weighing heavily on his mind again.

He approaches the mounds that protect the chambers where all of our ashes sit; rabbits race up and over the barrow, then stop, noses twitching, at Nick's approach. On special days the barrow is open but today, though special to those who knew me, is not such a day. Nevertheless, he steps inside the entranceway and leans his forehead against the coolness of the metal grille that forms the door. Entering the barrow may be off limits to unofficial visitors but it is still possible to see inside and the position of the sun, still gliding its leisurely way up to the peak of the day, means that in the first, smaller chamber the light glints off some of the niche doorways, including mine. Nick's eyes take in the family scene on the stained glass, and he smiles sadly. "Happy birthday, Ruth," he whispers, then casts his eyes around all of the space, sending silent greetings to everyone who resides here, before turning and walking to one of the benches.

"Such a lovely man," Teresa says as she joins me, watching Nick take a flask from his rucksack. He pours a cup of coffee, watching the tiny puffs of steam rise into the air, and he takes a sip. It's just the right side of scalding, and he feels the heat of it travel into him, taking the edge off the morning chill. It is going to be a hot day but right now the air is fresh and cool.

Joyous birdsong fills the air and Nick recognises the sound of the skylark, his eyes keenly scanning the fields to see one rise up from its ground dwelling. He is rewarded, and he can't help but smile. I share his happiness. I always loved having a summer birthday; as a girl it meant friends round to play in the garden. As a young woman, long nights out with light still visible in the sky as I traversed my way home. As I grew older, days out walking, with Graham or with friends. I had learned to take the day off work, and plan something for myself so that if nobody else had planned anything, I could still enjoy my day. It sounds self-indulgent but I think it's important to stop and appreciate your life, if you can, when you can. What better day to do that than your birthday?

"He really is," I agree with Teresa, a little late. She and I are taking in the view too; our view. We often wonder if this is it now, if this is where we will be forever. There could certainly be worse places. But Teresa thinks this is transient, though she knows not what comes next.

It works for now anyway; although I can see my family whenever I want, wherever I want, I like the fact that they make the effort to come here to see me, as they will later today, to self-consciously wish me a happy birthday. Their visits remind me that they are thinking of me, and I am still a part of their lives. *The love remains.* I remember hearing those words, and trying to make sense of them, though really they are so simple. It's like when somebody dies and people will say how much they loved them. But really, although the person might be in the past, the love has not ceased to exist. They love them in the present tense, still, and they will continue to love them in the future. The person has gone but the love remains.

A second skylark rises and a buzzard emerges from a distant tree, taking its time as it sails almost lazily overhead, in fact working hard, scanning the ground for a meal, but looking confident, relaxed, and entirely at ease.

Nick watches it, then he reaches into his bag and pulls out a banana, and then his phone. He peels back the thick skin of the banana and takes a bite then he unlocks his phone and he takes a photo, shooting just shy of the sun so that the light is blurred and the resulting shot is beautiful. He sends it to Claire.

That's where you are now? she asks, replying immediately, nursing a cup of tea in bed as she watches the breakfast news. **It's lovely.**

It is, he agrees. **I'll tell you about it later.**

I'm proud of him.

14

Nick is not the only one who's returned from London with a new friend.

Annie had been enjoying a long soak in the bath, washing off the perceived city grime, when her phone pinged. She wiped her soapy hands and reached for it, experiencing a little thrill when she saw the name Martin.

Just checking you got home alright x

She put the phone back down and smiled to herself. Shook her head at how less than twenty-four hours ago she'd been dancing with him, feeling his very solid, very reassuring, and quite thrilling, body next to hers. Trying to recapture the feeling, she considered how much she had wanted to be close to him, how she'd looked at his lips and imagined kissing him. Why had she never felt like this about anyone before? With Alex, things had been... nice. When he wasn't being annoying. Their sex had been ok, she thinks, but she could take it or leave it. Until now she'd assumed that was just another Annie Thing. Her aloofness following her through to the bedroom. Now, though, she wondered, was it actually an Alex and Annie Thing?

Even Martin's smell had been enticing. She tried to conjure it up in her mind, marvelling at how a couple of weeks earlier, her stomach was being turned by even the most mundane of scents.

She ran her hands over her body, feeling its softness through the suds, stroking the mound of her swelling belly. She could just see it rising slightly through the bubbles. Martin had made her feel desirable even though she was pregnant. That was something she would never have expected.

It was only much later, as she was sitting in her pyjamas, hair wrapped in a towel, that she thought she should probably message him back.

I did, thank you. Should she…? No. She couldn't add a kiss. It wasn't something she did. But as soon as she'd pressed send, she wondered if she should have done. Would her message look stark and cold? Maybe he'd take it as a brush-off. Perhaps that was it, she thought. Well, whatever, it was good to have met him. Great to know she could feel that way…

I'm glad to hear it. I enjoyed meeting you x

Her heart did a little skip. What was this? Well, I could tell her. This was her first real crush. It's taken over thirty years but she has got here eventually.

You too, she typed, then deleted. Then retyped.

Good journey back? X

It was, thank you.

Graham had upgraded their return tickets to first class, which was really sweet. They had sat in pairs; Annie with her dad and Tom with Kitty. The morning had consisted of a great hotel breakfast then a walk around Hyde Park, before heading back through the Underground network to Euston. By the time they got on the train they were all shattered and Graham had surprised them by going up to one of the staff on the platform and asking about an upgrade.

"Certainly sir. If you go to carriage B, there are seats in there. I'll ask the guard to come and find you."

"Yes, Dad!" Tom had said.

"Thanks, Dad," Kitty had hugged him.

Graham had led the way, a fully functioning dad again, and they'd trooped on board the train, grateful for the extra comfy seats and leg room.

"Have you had a good weekend, love?" Graham asked Annie once they were settled.

"Yes thanks. Have you?" Annie remembered to ask.

"It's been lovely." He rested his head back against the seat. "You know, I was dreading it. Not going away with you three, I hasten to add, but the date. The memories. It's like a lot of these firsts, the anticipation is worse than the days themselves. Though I think your mum's birthday will be hard."

They were both quiet, thinking back to my birthday last year. We knew it would be my last. Graham had tried to suggest that it might not be but I wasn't having it, and in fact we argued because of that. I just didn't see the point in being anything less than honest. And he'd wanted to take me out for lunch but I'd felt awful that day. I'd really tried to push myself; had a shower, got dressed, but I couldn't summon up the energy. I knew it hurt Graham but it wasn't like I was doing it on purpose and he realised that. Relented. Apologised, and insisted I return to bed, and we'd lain there together, thinking our own thoughts but looking at each other. It was so intimate, and raw, and heart-breaking.

In the evening, Tom had returned from work and Kitty and Annie and Alex came round and we'd sat in the garden and I'd managed to put on a better front for them, even managing a slice of the cake that Kitty had made. We'd sat out in the evening light until it had faded away, and when the children had gone Graham and I sat a little longer, me resting my head against him and pretending not to notice that he was crying.

Back to work tomorrow then? x

I had to hand it to Martin, he was committed to those kisses, despite the lack of reciprocation from Annie.

Yes.

I'm a bit nervous.

That was progress for my daughter. She had hesitated before sending that second message but decided it couldn't hurt. While the others were still dancing, Martin had taken her to the bar to get a drink and they'd sat for some time, talking about their lives and their work. She'd found herself telling him about the situation with Ryan Edwards, inwardly congratulating herself on having been open with Meg and now doing the same with this man she had only just met. Maybe it actually helped that they were disconnected from her everyday life. And, unlike her family, they had no preconceptions.

Annie was always an achiever and a worker. She pushed herself so hard to get top marks in her exams at school and at university. Driven and determined, she always knew the path she was going to take, following in her dad's footsteps. I had always assumed it was what she wanted and to a great extent it was but I've come to realise she has also been labouring under the misconception it is what was expected of her.

A part of Annie envies Tom and Kitty their freedom and their lack of focus (though both would object to that; it's just that Kitty's focus is her art and Tom's his music, and neither of those are bearing much fruit right now).

I get that x

Will they think I'm weak? Taking early maternity leave?

Does it matter what they think? x

It mattered very much to Annie what her colleagues thought of her, professionally at least. She was never going to be the popular one in the office but she was damn good at her job and she knew it. Her colleagues did too.

Martin is typing...

That message was displayed for a long time and Annie waited to see what he was going to say next. Eventually...

Honestly Annie, once you're out of there you won't look back. You've been there so long, it's become the main focus of your life and so you think that it matters, how these blokes perceive you. But who are

they, really, to you? Your boss, and the prick that's coming to steal your job. What does it matter, what they think? If you're really serious about going freelance, you give yourself the best chance to lay the foundations now. Once that baby comes along, your world will change again. Set yourself up now so you have a base for you and that little girl x

Martin had told Annie that he became a dad quite young and he is not particularly proud of his early years of fatherhood, having split from his children's mother when his younger daughter was two, throwing himself into work.

"I always told myself it was so I could be a Provider." He had puffed his chest out jokingly, poking fun at himself. "It was true, to an extent, but I loved work too and I loved the social life that came with it. Sales is a shiny world full of cash and incentives and heavy nights out with clients. That just doesn't sit well with a young family but at the time I was too young to see what a dick I was being."

How do you know it's a girl? Annie smiled as she pressed send, also neatly dodging the subject of her work.

Ah, my bad! Comes from being a father to two daughters! Anyway, don't change the subject. You going to do it, tomorrow? X

I think so. Yes.

Great! You can do it, Annie. And sounds like you've got a good family behind you for support. x

Everything's changing, she typed and sent it without really thinking.

I know. But that's not all bad. x

I guess. Annie's eyes had filled with tears then, at the thought of me. And she'd wondered what I'd think about everything. Her split with Alex; her pregnancy; planning to leave her job… meeting a strange man in London and trusting him with, well not quite her innermost thoughts, but trusting him.

I am beyond proud of you, Annie, I willed her to hear me; feel me, somehow, but I couldn't get through.

Thank you she sent. As an afterthought: **X**.

And down in his East London townhouse, Martin had smiled.

15

"This is amazing, Kitty!" Cecily hugs her boyfriend's sister as she looks around the space.

Kitty is one of four artists displaying their work at an exhibition not far from where she lives. It's being hosted at a new, small gallery, and her long barrow series takes up one whole wall.

"It's only a small thing…" Kitty smiles modestly, clutching her glass of wine and in truth feeling proud and nervous and as though she is on display herself. The local paper and radio station have sent journalists to cover the story and, though she keeps telling herself it's the same thing, it's only small…

"You've got to start somewhere," Tom voices her thoughts, kissing her on the cheek. "and this is a lovely space. They obviously know what they're doing."

Their eyes alight on Mo and Prim, the gallery owners, who are engaged in conversation with the radio journalist.

"Well, let's see. It's fun, anyway," Kitty says brightly, but Tom isn't fooled. He knows just how much this means to his sister.

The opening night has drawn quite a crowd too.

"Because nothing much happens round here!" Kitty laughs.

"Hey!" Meg, who has managed to convince one of the volunteers to watch the kennels for an hour or two, is resplendent in a pair of bright dungarees. "This is a bustling hotbed of creativity, thank you very much."

"Are you sure about that, Meg?" Annie asks, and everyone chuckles, their approval making her glow.

She's much happier these days, and more relaxed in her manner, though she's still on edge about her decision. In a few short weeks' time, she will be on maternity leave, and in another couple of months, she will be a mum. Maybe earlier, but she really hopes not. That would throw a spanner in the works.

"Hey, there's Tasha!" Kitty says. "She said she'd come, she doesn't live too far from here."

"Hi!" Tasha grins at them all. "This is Joao, my fiancé."

"Saw your band in London, man," Tom says, making his sisters share a grin. "You were awesome."

"Thanks, mate," Joao's accent is a mix of Brazilian and Cockney. Tasha hangs off his arm, smiling. "Hi Graham," she says, as Kitty's proud dad joins the group.

"Oh, hi, er…" he looks flustered.

"Tasha," Kitty reminds him.

"Yes of course, hi Tasha. Nice to see you. Here, Annie, I got you an orange juice." He hands her a glass.

"Kitty, we need you over here," Mo bustles up, smiling widely at them all. "Sorry to steal her away, guys. And if you don't mind moving through the room a bit, it's a little busier that we were expecting…"

"Of course," Graham says. "You must be really proud…"

But Mo has already gone and Graham's face turns red.

"Never mind, Dad!" Tom laughs. "Let's go and have a look around."

It's packed, and hot, in the gallery, and they don't stay too long, but Graham is gratified to see two of Kitty's pieces have stickers on them, to show they've been bought.

If only you were here to see this, Ruth, he thinks.

If only you knew. I stay close by his side and feel the same swell of pride at our daughter's success. Modest it may be, but as Tom says, you have to start somewhere.

One person Kitty hadn't expected to see there was Alex but he's come, and he's brought Donna with him. He kisses his soon to be ex-sister-in-law chastely on the cheek.

"Hi Alex," Kitty is at once awkward and touched that he's come. "I wasn't expecting you!"

"As if I'd have missed this!" he says, slightly awkwardly. "I'm really proud of you, Kitty. If I'm allowed to be?"

"You are! Oh Alex." The emotion of the evening sweeps Kitty with generosity. "I am really pleased you've come, thank you."

The three of them pause for a moment and look around, Kitty hearing the chatter and laughter that fills the room. "I can't believe this many people are here!"

"Why not?" asks Alex. "This is a great exhibition. You've done really well to get to this point, and who knows what comes next?"

"I love your paintings," Donna says shyly. "It must be really exciting seeing people buying them."

"It really is!" Kitty is glad that her family have already left by this point but she is pleased for Alex too. There is no reason he should be lonely and he's not a man that does well without a relationship. She hugs him, glad that Richard, one of the other artists, is waving her over. "I've got to go. It's lovely to meet you, Donna." She finds that she means it.

When she is finally free, Kitty meets up with Graham and the others at the Young Buck, the pub near the kennels. She is tired and her head hurts but she's also grinning from ear to ear and flushed with the success of the evening.

"Here, Kitty, let me get you a drink," her dad says, standing so she can sit down. He returns with a bottle of prosecco.

"Dad!" Kitty says, but she is delighted.

"It's not often your daughter has her first art exhibition," he shrugs. "And as your mum used to say, it's important to acknowledge the things worth celebrating."

So you did listen to me! I nudge softly against my husband and, just for a moment, I think he's felt something. He has a mental shake of his head and goes about pouring glasses for all of them, including a very small one for Annie. They are all staying in the rooms above the Young Buck, except Annie, who is driving herself and her sister back to Kitty's flat for the night.

"Cheers Kitty!" Tom raises his glass and the others follow suit, as Kitty's face blushes red. She hides her embarrassment with a sip of wine.

"It's brilliant, Kitty. Own it!" Cecily says.

"OK!" my younger daughter laughs. "I will. I sold all but two of my paintings," she admits.

"Well done," Annie puts her arm around her. "Really, Kitty. Well done."

"Thank you Annie." Slightly taken aback, Kitty looks at her sister.

"You're actually making your own dream come true," Annie says. "That is something to be celebrated."

"Definitely," says Tom. "Loads of people were admiring your work as well, you know, picking up your cards. It was so cool that Joao came too." He can't quite help mentioning Tasha's musician fiancé, whose band's own star is rising in a small way.

"It was really nice of them to come," says Graham. "I didn't know you'd kept in touch."

"Yeah well they're thinking of getting a dog, funnily enough, so I told them about the kennels and they've been across a couple of times. Then Meg had to tell them about tonight, of course!"

"She'd make a good agent," Cecily laughs.

"She would," Annie says, thinking of the role Meg's been playing in her own career change. She wants to tell them more about her own plans, as they are all together. She hasn't yet told Graham and she knows she must, but something is holding her back. She rubs her tummy briefly and keeps her counsel. This night is about Kitty, after all.

"So are they getting a dog?" Tom asks.

"I'm not sure yet, but I'll keep you informed." Kitty laughs and Annie does too.

"What?" asks Tom, in indignant little brother mode. "I'm just interested."

"Because of *Joao*," Kitty teases. "Watch out, Cecily, you've got competition."

Loyal Cecily just smiles and squeezes Tom's hand.

"Shut up, Kitty," says Tom, but he's grinning.

I watch them all, happy there in that moment, chatting and laughing, and winding each other up. If their thoughts go anywhere, it is to the future, wondering what it might bring. And for once I don't enter their minds. Just for a little while. And I don't mind at all. It's a good thing. It's how it has to be.

16

"What's all this?" Annie exclaims as she enters her office after lunch. Strung along the back wall is a jaunty row of bunting shaped like babygrows, and there is a pile of presents on her desk.

"We wanted to wish you well," says Becca from behind her. "We're excited for you."

Annie turns, stunned and not quite sure what to say. She had assumed her exit would be quiet and low key, and that people would be glad to see the back of her.

Some of her other workmates are gathering behind Becca.

"Good luck, Annie," says Gary, a father of three. "You'll need it!"

"Shh," Miriam says, nudging him. "What a thing to say! You'll love it, Annie. But I think you made a good decision taking some time off early. Get some sleep in now, while you can."

"I…" She realises they are smiling at her, which in itself is a surprise, having assumed that nobody at work really liked her. Even Jeff has joined them.

"Aren't you going to open your presents?" he asks.

"I... yes." Annie goes behind her desk and sits gratefully in her chair, pleased to have a bit of space between her and her colleagues, and something to do while they are all looking at her. But what if she doesn't like her gifts? That would look awful. She takes a subtle deep breath and composes her features so that she is ready to smile and exclaim how lovely everything is, then she opens the first present.

It is a starter pack for a baby. A set of beautifully soft babygrows, some muslins, bibs, bottles, something dubious called 'bedtime butter', a 'baby on board' car sign that Annie already knows she will not be using, and a mini first aid kit, which she thinks is a great idea. She looks up, sees the expectant faces, realises that she is smiling for real.

"This is lovely," she says, as she knows she is supposed to, but she really does mean it. "I wasn't expecting this at all."

"Annie," Jeff says, assuming the role of spokesperson, even though it was Miriam and Becca who had done all the organising and shopping, "you've worked here for years; we all respect you hugely, and want to wish you all the best for this new adventure. And we can't wait to meet your little one."

Just behind Jeff's shoulder, Annie sees Sam, the security guard, has sneaked up to join the gathering. He winks at her and she smiles back.

"Open the next one!" Becca says and Annie obediently picks up the next parcel, which is smaller and heavier. Carefully peeling away the paper, she sees a dark blue box. She slides off the lid to reveal a beautiful glass paperweight with a dried apricot-coloured rose set in the centre.

"I know it's not for the baby," Becca quickly explains, "but we wanted to get something just for you. We all admire you and how hard you work, and we want you to know that we'll be thinking of you, and hope we can come and meet your little one when you're ready. Don't let anyone rush you," she says sternly.

Becca's semi-maternal tone is warm and sincere, and tears prickle the back of Annie's eyes.

"I don't know what to say." She picks up the paperweight, feels its smooth solidity. She already knows where this will go; on the new desk she's bought and had delivered into the spare room, which is now the study, next to the baby's room. "It's lovely, and really kind of you."

There is a moment's silence then Sam pipes up, "Good luck Annie. We'll miss you."

There are murmurs of agreement and although Annie thinks they are probably just being polite, she is still touched. She opens her other presents, which include a lovely set of nursing pyjamas for her, and a soft blanket for the baby, and then Miriam brings in a tray of cakes, and some paper cups, and Annie's office is as full of people and voices as it's ever been. She sits back, sipping her squash, and sees Sam raise his cup to her before heading back downstairs. She raises hers back but he doesn't see. And she answers everyone's questions politely – no she doesn't know if it's a boy or a girl; yes she's sleeping OK, and no her feet aren't doing too badly in the heat, thank you. She's very glad that nobody asks to put their hand on her tummy as that is a step beyond what she can tolerate. But she is touched beyond words that they have thought of her, and want to give her a good send-off.

At the end of the day, Jeff calls her into his office. Ryan Edwards is there and they both look at her with smiles on their faces. It's hard to tell if they are genuine or smug.

"So, this is it," says Jeff. "It'll be strange not having you here. I think you made a wise decision though, taking maternity leave a bit earlier. It's hard work, having a baby. Different to all the hard work you've done here." He clearly thinks he is giving some meaningful advice. What does he think Annie is going to do in the next few weeks? Sit around watching *This Morning*?

"I'll take care of everything," Ryan says, and Annie thinks, *I bet you will.* "It's all in good hands, don't worry."

"Thanks," she says shortly. She lifts her arms slightly, indicating the bags of presents. "I'd better get these to the car."

Jeff leaps to his feet. "Do you want a hand?"

"No it's OK, I can manage." Annie squeezes a smile onto her face. "Thanks though."

He does at least open the door for her and she walks out, stopping at the reception desk to sign out one last time.

"This is it then," says Sam, as though he knows she is not planning to return.

"This is it," she agrees, and she looks at him and smiles.

"Don't be a stranger," he says.

"I'll try not to be."

"Can I help you with your bags?"

"Yes please Sam, that would be great."

They walk out to the car together. "I'll have to be quick, I already left my desk to see you opening the presents. I couldn't let you go without saying bye though." He surprises her with a hug. "Take care, Anne. You will be missed." Sam looks at her, saying the words firmly as though she needs to really hear them.

"Thank you, Sam. I'll be in touch."

"You'd better!"

Annie gets in the car and sees him dashing back to the office building. Annie looks it over, remembering all the hours she's put in here, and the first day when she came for an interview. She'd had such high hopes that she'd get to where Jeff is, but it seems this baby is determined to make her take a detour in her well-laid plans, and now she can see her life is heading in a different direction. It's at once scary and exciting. She starts the engine and drives out of the car park, heading towards the safety and security of her home yet at the same time into the wide open jaws of the unknown.

The next day is Saturday but this is no time to rest. Annie has set her new paperweight in pride of place on her beautiful polished oak desk, and her huge card from work is set beside her monitor. She has read and re-read the messages in there, ranging from 'Best wishes, Ryan' to a long missive on motherhood and how inspirational Annie has been, from Becca. The warmth contained in many of the messages has been another surprise for Annie. While she realises that the words may be more of a reflection of their generosity and spirit than their real feelings for her, she still finds herself wishing that she had known better how to be friends with them while she worked there. Because, all being well, and no reflection on them, she hopes very much that she will not be working with them again.

Turning on her laptop, she wipes away the smallest smudge that has somehow found its way onto her screen. She blows on the keyboard to dislodge any dust, then she wipes the surface of her desk to make sure the dust doesn't settle there. Then she logs into her computer and opens up her planner. Let the hard work begin.

It is lunchtime before she takes a break. In the hours beforehand, she has registered for self-employment, read up on what it means to be both employed, as she still is, and self-employed at the same time, reassuring herself there is no conflict there and no need for her to tell Jeff her plans.

She has also listed from memory as many clients she can think of who she has worked with, and highlighted those that did not come back. She cannot poach any existing clients of Jeff's, but she knows of others who have since gone elsewhere, and who she will make contact with once the working week begins.

Annie is determined to make her departure as clean and as ethical as she can. Even if she could approach any of her existing clients at work, she would not. This is her business and she is determined to act with integrity.

She has also begun to go through business listings and planning applications, making a note of any potentially suitable prospects. She wishes she had Miriam or Jamie with her to make the first call; that is going to be difficult. But this is it now; it's just her, and she is going to have to learn to be personable and approachable, and convincing. She is not a salesperson by any means and she has no doubt that this will be one of the hardest aspects of her work. So she will start with those who already know her and take it from there. All she needs is one or two good leads and she could be flying.

As she makes herself a bowl of pasta for lunch, she wonders should she tell potential clients she's about to have a baby? Yes! She scolds herself. Integrity, Annie. And to be honest it would be quite hard to hide it anyway. But she's worked it all out. These things take time to get going. Right now is about making contacts, making people aware that she is going to be working freelance (and hoping word does not reach Jeff's ears, though if it does she will deal with it).

Breaking her loyalty to the company she has worked at for years is not easy but she just has to remind herself of Ryan Edwards' self-satisfied face and the way his laughter rang alongside Jeff's around that empty office building. Loyalty should be a two-way street, she thinks, and Alex's face also springs to mind.

Men, she thinks, disparagingly, watching the tomato sauce bubble and spit in its pan. Her phone pings. It's Martin. *Maybe they're not all bad.*

How's your first day of freedom? Got your feet up? X

Not exactly. Annie turns the heat off under the saucepans, takes the pasta across to the sink and pours it carefully into the colander, watching the steam rise and create a thin, temporary layer of condensation on the window.

I knew it! You've been hard at work already? x

Time waits for no man. She imagines him smiling at that.

True. But just you make sure you look after yourself as well, OK? X

OK. I will. I promise. Annie decides to go and see Graham in the afternoon. She has done enough work for one day. Maybe they can go for a walk… visit the long barrow. It's been a while.

Good.

So what are you doing with your day? This is a relatively new development for Annie, remembering to ask other people about themselves. It's not that she doesn't care. It's just that she often doesn't think.

Got a family party. Daughters and all today. I wish you could come. x

Really? I'd be awful! Awkward. She shudders at the thought of having to meet a whole new group of people. But she likes that he's said that.

Martin sends a laughing emoji. Annie is not an emoji type of person but again she feels good. She likes the thought of making him laugh.

Maybe another time? x

Maybe.

X

They leave it there and she grates some cheese onto her pasta, watching with satisfaction as the little curls melt onto the hot red sauce. A sprinkling of salt and a grind of pepper, and she's good to go. Annie sits at her dining table in her empty house, opens her book to the place she has marked, and settles down to enjoy her lunch, luxuriating in her solitude.

17

I always used to find the end of summer difficult. Somehow, even after many years, I could never believe that I could be happy during the colder, darker months. I always thrived in the heat and those long daylight hours, loving languid days relaxing in the garden or lying on the beach.

Last summer I knew it was not only the season that was coming to a close but that my time on Earth was not going to last much longer either. My body had shrunk, revealing its fragile, bony frame just below the surface, and I was struggling to stay awake. Even when I was sleeping I couldn't escape the pain, though I did have vivid dreams taking me elsewhere, away from the torment of the illness and the torture of seeing the expressions on my family's faces when they looked at me, no matter how hard they tried to hide their feelings.

This year, Kitty is feeling it. She's on a downward trajectory at the moment, my middle child. Happy for Tom that he's found Cecily but missing his company. Those two were always close and she has been his default go-to for years – sharing jokes, Facebook posts and TikToks. Now his mind goes to his girlfriend instead and while he is aware, and tries not to leave Kitty out, he is in the throes of early love. He is desperate not to mess this up, especially as he already nearly did, once.

Kitty too is painfully aware of Mavis' fragility. Meg has pointed it out, trying to keep her friend and employee on the level with what to expect. Mavis can still get about but it's clear that she is sore. She will valiantly try and join Graham on his potters round the garden but a walk is really too much for her these days. Kitty knows this without Meg having to highlight it but she doesn't really want to face it. *Haven't I had enough to contend with?* she thinks but she knows that when it comes to it, the responsibility is going to lie with her.

Mavis, who was my puppy, a present for my sixtieth birthday, is like one last link to me, Kitty thinks, not seeing that she herself is and always will be a link to me. Just like Tom and Annie, and Annie's baby when she arrives.

Nothing can break our bond, I try to tell her. *Nothing.*

It just feels like everything is changing around Kitty and like she is losing control. She throws herself into her painting, which is seeing the benefit of her anguish as she becomes bolder and more expressive, losing herself in the colours and shapes. Trying somehow to convey this mixed-up mess of thoughts and feelings in the one place she is free to express herself.

Because at work she has to think of the dogs, and has to present a professional front. At our house, she has to put her own feelings on the back-burner and try to keep Graham going. With Annie, she is still reeling from what happened with Alex, and still feeling guilty, though her sister has genuinely put it all behind her. That is old news. Water under the bridge.

And Tom – well she's happy for him but if she is honest she's still a little bruised from their argument too. She does not want to rock that boat again. She can't afford to fall out with any of these people who are the significant others in her life, she thinks self-pityingly, sure that she is never going to find love again and not sure that she ever really did. I agree. She may have loved Olly, but he did not love her. He didn't know how to. And really, what kind of love is that?

As the air takes on that unmistakeable yet subtle morning chill, Kitty is acutely aware that autumn is on its way and this year it brings with it not just that back-to-school feeling that has never quite left her but memory upon memory of this time last year. The feelings that re-awaken are sharp, piercing, going deep into her as she remembers.

In this year of firsts, this next event is the one they have dreaded the most. The first anniversary of my death. What they hadn't seen coming was the anniversary of my final days and as each one of those comes along, it drags forgotten pain to the surface.

A year to the day since Justine came up to visit for one last time. I was looking forward to seeing my old friend, though I knew of course the significance of her visit as well. Kitty helped me get ready; washed my hair for me, got me some of the new clothes Graham had bought – two sizes smaller than I would normally have, and I'd protested, thinking it was a waste of money but not wanting to spell that out to him. I was glad of the bright stripey top that day though as I could put my best face on for Justine and try to convince myself and everyone else that I felt a little bit like my old self.

Kitty remembers this day now and how grateful I was for her help. She remembers too how she sat with Justine after lunch while I slept, unable to stay awake even though I desperately wanted to. In the end they had to gently pull me from my sleep because Justine had to leave again and they knew I would be so angry if I'd missed all chance of some time with her.

She told me about her family, showed me pictures of her daughter's two boys, and I knew she was worrying I'd feel cheated, that I never got to have grandchildren of my own, but I was genuinely filled with happiness for her. Life, life, life. It had taken on such value to me and I was glad of it in whatever shape or form. Happy to see those images of the two little boys with their chubby legs and faces, their whole lives ahead of them.

And Graham had made a pot of tea, but was gone for so long that Kitty went to see what was going on; found him fretting in the kitchen, in pieces. "Come on Dad," she'd said kindly, taking over the tea-making, getting down the best cups and saucers because what on earth were we saving them for? Tipping a packet of biscuits onto a plate, arranging them in a spiral because it felt comforting. Bringing it all out into the garden with a smile on her face and just stopping herself in time from saying 'Shall I be Mother?' for fear of upsetting me, that I could no longer fulfil that same role.

And she was there for me after Justine had to go, my friend's face pulled tight with emotions she was trying to hide as she said her goodbyes and hugged me then walked away then dashed back and hugged me again. Graham walked her to the car and I could hear their voices murmuring on the driveway, and I knew they were talking about me. Of course they were, but it stung nevertheless, like I was a child left out of a friendship group. That was my husband, that was my friend, and now it felt like they'd turned their backs on me and locked me out.

I didn't give in to tears many times in front of anyone else but that day I did, and Kitty held my hand, then held me, and I cried at the anticipation of her grief, at the knowledge I'd said my last farewell to my best friend, and at the utter bittersweetness of life, when I'd had so much, and so many wonderful people around me, and I should have been able to just appreciate that I had been so lucky when so many people in the world have such a terrible time of things, but all I wanted was more. And despite my good fortune it felt unfair and I allowed myself to think what I had warned myself not to: Why me?

Kitty's eyes overflow now as she remembers that day, and her sobs come in huge gasps that wrack her body. Although she allows herself time to cry, as she had in her hotel room in London, she rarely gives in to this depth of feeling and I'm glad that she does now, though it pains me to see it. And then, her mind plays that little trick it has of surveying the scene, like it's looking in on her, and she feels like she's being watched, and imagines an outsider seeing her, like she's on a stage or a screen, and it pulls her up short.

Just let yourself feel it, Kitty, I try to tell her, but already she is pulling herself together, wiping her nose on the back of her hand, almost laughing at herself. And then her phone goes, and she sees it is Tom.

"Alright sis?" he asks.

"Yeah," she half-laughs, half-sniffles.

"It sounds like you've got a cold," he says.

"I'm alright," she tells him. "How are you?"

"Yeah, good thanks," he says vaguely. "Listen,

Cecily had an idea, with Mum's anniversary coming up and the weather looking nice for a few days. She thought we could go to the seaside, on one of your days off. What do you think? It doesn't have to be the – you know, the exact date, because that's close to Annie's due date anyway. We should go while we have the chance!"

"I'll check my days off," Kitty says, "that sounds nice. You mean with Dad and Annie too?"

"Of course. And Mavis."

"I'm not sure she's up to it," Kitty says.

"But we can't leave her. And we can take it easy. You know she loves the beach."

"True." Kitty muses how they could make this work, a part of her marvelling at how just minutes ago she was lost in great heaving sobs and now she's planning a day at the coast. "OK. It sounds good."

"Great! I'll speak to Dad. Can you ask Annie?"

"Sure."

"Cool. I'll drop you a line in a bit."

He hangs up, pleased with himself and with Cecily. He's lucky to have her, in so many ways, and especially right now as she's helping him navigate through the twists and turns of these difficult days.

18

"Come on, Dad!" calls Tom, getting into the car and doing a very passable impression of Graham from the past, impatient to get on the way for family holidays, drumming his hand on the steering wheel while I conducted a last-minute check of everything in the house, squirting toilet cleaner into the loos and making sure there were not unwashed cups or plates squirrelled away anywhere, biding their time. I'd more than once discovered a mouldy mug worthy of penicillin status under Tom's bed.

"Coming!" Graham says amiably. It's funny how since I've died he's somehow more relaxed; more accepting somehow. Happy to be shepherded along and organised. When Tom suggested this day at the beach, he'd said, "Ooh yes go on then, that sounds nice. We could get fish and chips—"

His eyes had shone, from the numerous memories of me and him doing this together. Every summer we'd head across to the North Wales coast, at least once, for a walk on the beach and a swim in the sea, and end up with fish and chips, steaming hot and eaten out of their papery wrappings under the blue sky and the keen eyes of watchful gulls, or inside a steamy car, depending on our luck with the weather.

"I know, Dad," Tom had said kindly. "Mum would love to think that we're doing this, though."

How many times have I been mentioned like this? My wishes and intentions mentioned in order to make something feel a bit more acceptable, or bearable? Tom is right, of course, but even if he wasn't, what would it matter? This is their life now, I have withdrawn from it, and whatever makes them happier is fine by me.

Graham lowers himself into the passenger seat. "Are you sure you don't want to sit in the front, Annie?" He turns guiltily to his pregnant daughter.

"No, I'm fine Dad," she says, and shoots him a smile that she hopes is reassuring.

Tucked between Kitty and Annie on the back seat is Mavis, already curled up and ready to sleep. She's just happy to be with her people. I experience an unusual stomach churn, wishing I was with them in person; I could have just about fitted between my two girls on the back seat, and Mavis could have slept on me. I wouldn't have minded. Actually, perhaps I would, at one time. It would not have been the most comfortable of journeys. Now, though, the idea of all that physical closeness pulls at me. The feeling of my daughters' very real, warm bodies either side of me and my ever-loving dog curled up on my lap. The camaraderie of all of us in the same car together – all too old now for the silly bickering of the past. What would I give for that?

I did always know to appreciate it. Well, maybe not always. But I did try to look ahead, when the children were little, and even more as they became older and bigger and grew into their personalities; to see a future not all that far away, when they'd left home, and I'd try to remind myself, in the depths of a family argument or a long, irritable car journey, that these together-times were to be cherished. If that makes me sound like some kind of saint, I definitely wasn't. I could often feel my hackles rising and shoulders tensing, and I'd have to take deep breaths at times – and that wasn't always effective. But I did make myself stop and think when I could, and try to remind myself that we all had a perspective, and different feelings, and that was why family life could be a challenge. But I wouldn't have changed it for anything.

Annie dozes as Kitty checks her phone, and Graham and Tom talk about cricket. Every now and then, a thought will shoot into Annie's mind, like an arrow piercing her subconscious and bringing her back to reality. This whole freelance thing is exciting her but fraying her nerves. And she still hasn't told Graham what she's doing, or Alex – not that it's his business anymore. Except she does need to be able to support their child.

You both need to be able to do that, Martin had counselled last night. They message each other regularly; most nights, in fact. **It's your joint responsibility x**

He has never stopped sending her kisses, though she rarely responds in kind.

But I ended things with Alex.

You ended your marriage, not his parenthood. Trust me. I know what I'm talking about x

Martin is a good, stand-up, reliable and generous father, but he did not live in the family home while his children were growing up. And their mum has harboured resentment towards him, though she's mellowed in recent years, especially since she's found a lovely partner.

But I need to know I can do it, alone.

You don't. You won't be. You have a family who adore you, and it sounds like Alex is reliable. You won't have to do anything alone x

Annie considered this, knowing Martin was right. But if she could only be assured her business will work and she will make an income enough for her and her child, she will rest better, assured that if everybody else was to fall away, she would still be ok.

You need to remember to trust people x Martin sent, without waiting for a reply.

It was funny how open she found herself being with this man, and if she pushed herself to try and remember his face, Annie found she sometimes couldn't. She had to look at his profile picture to remember him, and then she'd get a little glimpse of those feelings again, and find herself wishing he was with her in person. Except, she was finding, it was easier to be open and honest when corresponding like this, through the portal of her mobile phone screen.

Thank you, she sent. **X**

Any time x

It had made her smile, and sent a little thrill through her, as she imagined him smiling too, and remembered him looking at her in that club, and his hands on her waist... Was it just hormones playing havoc with her? She shook her head at the thought, half trying to expel the images, half very much wanting them to stay.

"What are you smiling about?" Kitty's voice breaks into her sister's thoughts.

"What? Am I smiling?"

"Yes!" Kitty laughs, with some idea of the reason behind that smile.

"Oh, erm…" Annie ruffles Mavis' fur with a guilty look but Kitty just smiles back, puts a reassuring hand on her arm, and Annie relaxes.

"First one to see the sea gets a pound coin!" Graham exclaims now.

"I thought it was 50p?" Kitty asks.

"That's inflation for you!"

They are not far from the coast now, in a familiar spot from where they all know that it won't be long before the coast swings into view.

"I see it!" says Tom.

"No you don't, you can't, that's the clouds," Kitty protests.

"No, it's the sea."

"Damn."

"That's a pound for Tom," says Graham. "Well done, son."

They fall quiet for a while as Tom takes the turn off the main road, heading down towards the quieter lanes and the little beach Graham and I discovered in the early days of our marriage. We had come hiking for a few days and a little old local woman had told us about this place, making us promise not to tell too many people. Now it's been broadcast on social media, the supposedly secret location that everybody knows about, it can be disappointingly busy. But today, my family are happy to see as they pull into the small parking area, there are not many people here.

They pile out of the car, Tom, Kitty and even Annie swept up in a wave of excitement at the familiar smells and sounds of the sea, and the gulls, and the strength of the breeze rushing to greet them. Kitty helps Mavis down gently and our lovely old dog raises her nose into the air, regally taking in the scents of this place she loves.

Graham takes his time getting out, allowing himself a few moments to stop and consider the many occasions we have been here before, memories fanning out like a pack of cards. Our first visit and then our second, later the same day, and our first experience of skinny-dipping. It had been a clear, starry night and the moon had shone down on our pale skin, and we'd looked at each other, shivering with the cold of the water and the desire we felt, moving towards each other amidst the gently rocking waves.

Other visits followed, none as romantic as that first one, but over time we came when I was pregnant, then with baby Annie, then toddler Annie and baby Kitty... then Tom came along and as the children grew we'd bring cricket sets and boules, and cool boxes, and elaborate picnics that could last the whole day. Sometimes we'd invite friends to join us but my favourite times were when it was just the five of us. And each of those days would end the same way, driving to the nearby town, buying fish and chips, and sitting on the harbour wall, sun-soaked, tired and utterly fulfilled, at peace with each other. Just happy together.

Mavis goes gamely with them as they cross the sands, heading straight to the seashore, Tom hopping along and taking off shoes and socks on the way. She is tired, though, already, by the time they reach the sea, and it's not lost on any of them – even Annie – how in times past she'd have been there before them, probably having run that distance three of four times over, barking as she zoomed between her people and the water. Barking again at the waves, warning them to keep back, satisfied that it was working as each body of bubbling water would rush towards her then beat a retreat.

Today, she is not barking. She is not running. Her legs and hips are sore and her body and mind are tired. But she is happy. I whisper to her, *Good girl, Mavis*, and I'm rewarded by a turn of her head; a wag of her tail. Kitty sees it, and somewhere in her subconscious something pings, but she's not ready to put those things together just yet.

"I'll stay here with Mavis," she calls to the others over the noise of the waves and the breeze. It is stronger down near the shoreline. "You go ahead."

The tradition is a full length of the beach, to the rocks and back, before returning to settle and have a picnic, and a swim. Kitty can see that a long walk will do Mavis no good today.

"I'll stay with you," Tom says. "We can do some skimming."

"You know I'm rubbish at skimming!" Kitty says.

"Yes. I could do with a laugh."

Kitty pushes him, and he half stumbles into the water. He pushes her back.

"Hey, careful! I've still got my shoes on!"

"Take them off then."

These two have reverted to their childhood selves, as they tend to do when they are on the beach. It could be very hard to keep them out of the water.

"You up to the walk, Annie?" Graham asks.

"Yes," Annie says proudly, absolutely unable to admit that a pregnancy might have any effect on her physically.

"Lovely." He smiles as his eyes scan his daughter, taking in the curve of her belly and the healthy pink colour of her rounded cheeks, which he thinks is becoming, though he would never say that out loud. Not to Annie, anyway.

They head on their way in companionable silence, Graham's eyes scanning the sea and alighting on a guillemot. He has always loved the seabirds, and thanks to him I came to love them too. Theirs is a different world to ours, spanning the realms of the living and the – well, whatever I am now. They know us all.

Annie, though, has her mind on other things. She still has not told Graham her plans, and she knows it's time. She takes a breath.

"Dad," she puts a hand on his arm.

Graham, half-startled by the unexpected physical contact, turns to her. "Everything OK, Annie?"

"Yes, it's… well, mostly. I mean…" This is dithery for Annie. It sets alarm bells ringing in Graham's mind.

She sets off again, at a bit of a pace, and he quickly catches up. "Is the baby OK?"

"Yes," she says, half annoyed that the baby is the first thing he thinks of. Is that all that is important about her now? "It's not the baby. It's work."

"Oh?" Graham is all ears now, relieved that his grandchild is alright and keen to hear whatever it is that is bothering Annie about her career. He has always been so proud she followed his footsteps and she's done so well for herself. He's happy to advise her if he can.

"I'm leaving the firm," she says quietly, just as a gust of wind whips past, carrying her words away.

"What was that?" he asks jovially. "It sounded like you said you were leaving the firm!"

"I am."

"What?" He is astounded. "Why would you do that? You don't have to give it up you know, to be a mum. We can work it out. I can help. I–I'd love to." A small part of him is panicking, having been looking forward to looking after the baby for Annie. It's something he knows will keep him going, on the dark days. And another small part of him wants to make up for his lack of contact with the girls when they were babies. He was around more for Tom when he was small, when I was ill, but he was notably absent in our daughters' early years.

"You still can, Dad. I'm not giving up work."

"Oh, so...?" He is at once relieved and confused.

"I'm setting up on my own."

"You're – how? What? I'm not sure that's a good idea, Annie."

Blunt yet piercing at the same time, Graham's reaction was expected but still painful. "But that's what I'm doing, Dad. It's why I've taken maternity leave early. I'm already speaking to potential clients and it's going well, actually."

"But what about your pension, Annie?" Graham stops and looks at her, his mind going predictably – and admittedly sensibly – to the steady stability of employment. The regular wages, the pension contributions, paid annual leave, and even sick leave.

"I can sort that out," she says, irritably. "People do, you know."

"Regular income?" he asks, as they walk on.

"That's the scary part," she admits.

"I don't know, Annie, are you sure this is a good idea?"

"I don't know either," she flashes angrily. "But I'm jumping before I'm pushed."

"What do you mean?"

She tells him about Ryan Edwards, though she's almost embarrassed about this. Nobody ever tried to replace Graham at work. But Graham's not a woman. Parenthood was never a threat to his work productivity and effectiveness. It rarely is when it comes to men.

"It sounds like they're just covering themselves," he says. "They need somebody to do your work while you're away."

"You make it sound like I'm going on holiday, Dad," she says. "And they're not just covering themselves. Believe me. This kind of thing happens all the time."

Graham considers the women he worked with in his career, reflecting how none of them ever reached his position of seniority, and how many of them in fact left when children came along, or reduced their hours; limited their own career prospects for the good of their families. The secretary whisks through his mind, stirring up guilt within him. Not just towards me but to her as well. She left her job as a result of what happened between them, while he carried on as before, climbing the greasy ladder and eventually making it to the top, completely unhindered by that ill-advised affair.

Annie, meanwhile, is feeling the anger building inside her, rising unstoppably; the resentment that has been simmering away for a long time heating up. Images of Jeff and Ryan bubble to the surface. Their smug, self-satisfied faces and the echoes of their laughter ringing around the offices where Annie has put in more than her fair share of hours over the years. And Alex. Stupid, soft Alex, so needy and desperate for affection and approval that he sought it in her sister, of all people – Kitty, when she was grieving and raw and vulnerable. And now, while Annie is still carrying his child, he's already found a replacement wife. *Donna*, she thinks meanly. Probably a carbon copy of Celia. Because that's what he's been looking for. A second mummy. Somebody to look after him, tend to his every whim. Why in the world he ever set his sights on Annie, she has no idea. She was never going to be that person. All of this bursts out of her now, finding its target in her father, as representative of all men.

"You never had to think about this!" she shouts. "You had Mum. You could just head straight back out to work as if nothing had changed."

"That's not fair, Annie," Graham says, but he's turned pale. Does she know? Do all his children know, about his affair? That he betrayed me? He looks around, from Annie then back to Kitty and Tom, who are thankfully far enough away not to have noticed the argument. No, he thinks, knowing I would never have told them about that. I would never have wanted to discolour our children's image of their dad. Knowing this, and feeling a little bit guilty at the relief that seeps into him, he takes courage, finds strength in his argument. "And if you hadn't chucked Alex out, *you'd* still have *him*."

Annie feels like she's been kicked in the teeth. And she, like me, has a misguided loyalty, though it's also protection of Kitty that prevents her from telling their father how things really went with Alex.

Graham thinks he's gone a step too far. "I don't know," he says gruffly. "I just would have thought you and Alex could work things out, for the sake of the baby."

For the sake of the baby, I think. When did Graham become so sanctimonious? And he doesn't even really like Alex! Has never thought he is good enough for our daughter.

"Thanks a lot, Dad." Angry tears shine in Annie's eyes and the bubble of anger bursts. "I was hoping for a bit more support, you know."

Seeing her like this; those rare tears, has the same effect on Graham's self-righteous rage. His shoulders slump and he puts his hand on her arm, stops her in her tracks and turns her to face him. "I just think – oh, I'm sorry Annie, of course I'll support you. You know that. In any way I can."

She manages a small smile but inwardly she's in turmoil. Graham's reignited the smouldering doubts she has herself and they're starting to burn again. Is she mad, leaving a regular, steady job, when she's about to become a mum as well? And she's just split up with her husband too. Her whole world is turning on its head.

You are absolutely right, Annie, I try to soothe her, but there is no way I am getting through to her. The two of them continue their walk in uncomfortable silence until Graham feels bound to talk again.

"Honestly, Annie, you know I'll support you. I can't wait to do some childminding for you. Honestly, you tell me when you need me, and I'll be there."

"Thank you Dad."

"And you give it a go, this freelance thing, and if it all comes crashing down you know I can give you a hand, financially. You don't have to worry."

She manages another smile but Graham has missed the point yet also hit upon one of her greatest worries. This isn't a little hobby she's trying out – it's a new way of working. It's her career, which she has put so much time and effort and energy into. She has no intention of it coming crashing down but, a little voice says, what if it does? She cannot countenance that idea.

Graham feels better now, as he walks along beside his daughter. They reach the rocky outcrop at the end of the beach and stop for a while, watching a pair of cormorants spread their wings, standing perfectly still on the dark, barnacle-covered rocks, meditating.

But while her dad feels better, Annie's stomach is churning, with the worry and anxiety she has been keeping at bay. *It's a bad idea,* she's thinking. *A stupid idea. What on earth am I doing?*

19

"You're still looking for your dad's approval!" Meg laughs.

"No I'm not," Annie says, irritated by this but still glad Meg has called. She does now, every couple of weeks, and at first Annie had thought she was just being kind, checking in on her, but she's come to realise that Meg actually likes her. She seems to be phoning because she just wants to chat. This is a new one for my daughter.

"You are. We all are. I mean, not your dad specifically, but our parents. My god, my mum and dad were a nightmare, when I told them what I was planning to do. Still are, to be honest. From their point of view, I've given up a great job – or great income at least – to live in poverty among a bunch of smelly hounds."

"You have," Annie says, and is surprised by Meg's laughter.

"Thanks, mate."

"Well…" Annie thinks what to say, seeing that perhaps she could have reacted a bit differently.

"No, I like that about you, your honesty. And yes, you're right. That is exactly what I've done. And I get why it bothers them. When I was in a relationship, living in a nice flat, with regular holidays, they could relax. I was sorted. I guess when you're a parent it's all you want, to know your kids are OK. I had flown the nest and settled down and had no financial worries. Now, I've chucked it all up in the air and I'm almost living hand to mouth most of the time. I get why it bothers them. I'm their little girl, aren't I?"

"But you're an adult," Annie says. "A grown woman."

"Yes, I am. You know that, and I know that, but I'm also still their daughter. I get it now. But I can't let it change how I do things. This is a growing experience, Annie, learning to cut those apron strings. Choosing to claim your life as your own."

Annie is quiet for a moment. Contemplating how her father's pride in her has been a driving force. "I see what you mean."

"We can't just live for our parents' approval, we're not kids anymore."

But this shared interest with Graham and their aligned careers has always put Annie in a privileged position with her father. He understands this side of her and it's a rare thing for her to feel understood. It's also a rare thing for her to feel appreciated more than her siblings, and she knows she is to some extent her father's favourite. It's hard to put a value on that, in a world where she usually feels misunderstood at best and shunned at worst.

"Graham's a lovely man. He's just trying to make sure you're OK. But he's never done what you're doing. He was loyal to the company he worked for and it paid off, but it's not that simple now, and especially if you're a woman. Honestly Annie, you are doing the right thing."

"Do you really think so?"

"I know so. That's not to say it'll be easy. And I know I have no idea about parenthood so that's going to complicate matters, I'm sure, but you can do it, Annie. Honestly. You have the drive, the brains, the experience, and you're unencumbered by a relationship now. Go for it, and feel confidence in yourself. You don't need approval from anyone else."

She sounds very wise x

Martin is also building Annie back up, throwing water over her smouldering doubts.

I think maybe she is.

It's only natural you'll have a wobble, and you'll have more. It would be weird if you didn't. And Meg's right, your dad's just being a dad. But it doesn't mean he's right x

But you're a dad. And you think you're always right.

She smiles a little as she sends this, imagining his reaction. Gets a little laughing face emoji back before his typed reply.

Well yeah, of course I'm always right. But it doesn't mean anyone else is. Look Annie, it's a tough one. I don't want to advise you what to do. It's your career. Your life. But right now you're OK, aren't you? You haven't given in your notice at work. You're on maternity leave. You can see how things pan out. I mean, you can't underestimate how much your baby is going to take over your life while you get the hang of it – being a mum, I mean – but you have time to do that. And you can fall back on your job if you need to. Keep that option open for now x

This 'wait and see', up in the air, situation is a challenge for Annie, who likes to know where she stands, and what she might expect. She is now facing a future as a mother, which she knows she has no idea about no matter how many books she has read, and on top of that she is trying to manage a fledgling small business, with no guaranteed clients or even income. This is indeed a growing experience, as Meg put it.

Thank you Martin x

Annie is more forthcoming with the kisses on her messages these days, just like she is braver with trying to make him laugh; teasing him, even. She sits back on her sofa, hands resting on her stomach, contemplating how within the space of one year she has lost me, she has lost her marriage, she might be losing her position at work… yet she has gained a friend – two, even. Meg and Martin. She's never really had friends before, her brother and sister being her main ports of call – and me, of course. Now she has two friends, and soon she will have a baby as well. And her own business, if she can just stay the course. It is dizzying, all this change. She slowly lays her head back against the cushions and closes her eyes, gently applying the brakes to the merry-go-round of thoughts and fears.

20

The argument with Annie has shaken Graham and it's kicked him into action.

After their trip to the beach, and the traditional chippy tea on the harbourside, a shattered Mavis lying at their feet (though not too tired to tuck into the piece of fish they bought her), my family had piled back into the car and headed home.

"Shall we stop and see Mum on the way back?" Tom had asked. His sisters looked at each other, irked as ever by his turn of phrase.

"Yes, it would be nice to go to the long barrow," Kitty said pointedly.

"It'll be dark by the time we get there," said Graham. "Or nearly, at least."

"It doesn't matter, does it?" Annie asked, unusually open to an impromptu idea. "I think it would be nice. Just for a few minutes."

They'd all felt my absence that day, and again once they were tucked into the family car, Graham driving the homeward stretch and Annie in the front seat where in years gone by it would have been me.

"But Mavis…" Graham was finding that for some reason he was reluctant to go to the long barrow, perhaps feeling a residual guilt from having memories of his affair raked up again.

"We can drive up to the barrow, Dad," Tom said. "Just this once. I'll clear it with Cecily. Nobody will be around. Then Mavis won't have to walk very far. She could even stay in the car."

"I don't know…"

"Come on, Dad!" Kitty, sitting behind him, put her hands on his shoulders. "It'll be an adventure!"

Something about that made him laugh and, knowing he was outnumbered, he caved in. "Go on then. As long as Cecily says it's OK."

Tom swiftly messaged his girlfriend, glad of a valid excuse, and she messaged back equally swiftly. "It's fine! Let's do it!"

So under cover of near darkness, Graham had driven slowly along the bumpy track, swearing at the occasional scraping sounds on the underside of the car, headlights on full beam.

"What if they think we're poachers?" Kitty had for some reason felt the need to whisper. "Come out with their shotguns?"

"This isn't a Roald Dahl book!" Tom laughed.

They reached the small parking area and Kitty gently roused Mavis from her sleep. My beautiful dog startled, and tried to move her stiff joints. "Here, sweetie," Kitty gently slid her hands under Mavis' belly. "Let me help you." She lifted her out of the car and Mavis shook her long ears, raising her nose to the air.

"Rabbits?" Tom asked her, ruffling the top of her head.

No, I thought. *Me.* This time Mavis knew I was there. We connected in a way we hadn't before. And I knew what it meant, but once her joints had loosened she trotted gamely alongside Kitty towards the barrow and waited while Graham punched in the numbers, before realising the padlock was already loose. "Somebody's left it unlocked," he tutted, but then came a slightly nervous "Hello?", echoing around the chambers.

My children and husband all jumped.

"Hello?" Annie called back bravely.

A beam of light swung round from within the second chamber, blinding them. There was the crunching of footsteps on gravel. "Sorry!" There was apologetic laughter and the light went off, plunging everyone into darkness. "It's me, Derek."

"Derek!" Kitty, relief evident in her voice, laughed, while Annie tried to remember who Derek was.

I looked at Teresa and smiled. Her son had been in the long barrow for an hour or so, having walked up at sunset and then settled into the peace of the place, sitting quietly, quite alone.

Kitty switched her own phone light on but shone it at the floor so only a soft glow was emitted into the space.

"Sorry I scared you!" Derek smiled at her, then at the others.

"That's OK mate," Tom said cheerily, thinking again of how ill-suited the name was to this man who was probably Annie's age at most. To Tom, the name Derek conjured up images of brown slacks and beige shirts, socks with suspenders... He imagined Annie calling her baby Derek and smothered a laugh.

"I was about to leave anyway," Derek said, though he hadn't really been thinking of this at all. He'd been half thinking he might curl his slender body along one of the curved seats in the smaller chamber and sleep there, letting the sun wake him in the early hours of the morning, slicing seductively through the dark sky and flooding the chamber with light.

"Not on our account," Graham said.

"Oh no, it's fine," Derek assured him. "I'll leave you to it." And he smiled politely at them all, his eyes meeting Kitty's last, as she stepped back into the outside world to let him pass at the exact moment a tawny owl called from the oak tree beyond the pond, answered moments later by her mate in a matching oak across the fields.

Kitty watched Derek walk away, then turned her eyes to the indigo sky, where the stars were beginning to announce themselves. "Come on Mavis," she said, and they walked inside the barrow slightly after the others, joining them in front of my niche. Graham took Annie's hand and she in turn took Tom's, who held his hand out for Kitty as she joined them. One by one, I flickered the lights on their phones and they looked at each other. Tom raised his eyebrows at Kitty, who shrugged her shoulders in return but Annie shook her head. Then she freed her hand from Graham's and touched her tummy, where her baby tumbled in protest at her mother's refusal to see what was right in front of her.

Graham looked from one child to the next. *But what if?* he thought. And his hand still felt the memory of Annie's in his, and I placed my own hand there instead, and stroked his fingers, as I had used to. He felt the shadow of it, and shook his head. *But what if...?* he thought again.

Through the twilight and into the darkness, the veil becomes thinner, and in the barrow it can be almost opaque. Mavis turned her head to Graham and me, and wagged her tail, but nobody saw it.

Yes, Graham, I said to him, though he wasn't ready to hear it. But still, his eyes on the stained glass of my niche door and the figures depicted there, his gaze fell on the mother, then he looked to his daughter standing next to him, her hand still on her belly, and he saw that he needed to step up, and step in. He put his arm around Annie's shoulder and she stiffened for just a moment, then relented, and laid her head against his shoulder, supported.

Now, Graham is all go. While Annie sits in her office – ever more uncomfortable as the baby expands daily, filling the space inside her greedily then stretching it ever further, elbowing and kneeing her while she speaks to potential clients and creates complex spreadsheets and project plans – Graham works at her house. He starts with the guttering, clearing it all, and straightens a couple of loose tiles on the roof. He fixes stair gates at the top and bottom of the stairs even though Annie assures him it will be a while before they're needed. He persuades her to let him buy a second-hand cot and spends a pleasant day in the garden, sanding it down and painting it a beautiful blue called Denim Drift, as chosen by Annie.

"But you don't know if it's a boy... do you?" Graham had asked.

"No! But I do know that I like the colour blue," Annie had said sternly. "And I'm a girl."

"OK, I take your point!" Graham grinned.

"Good!" But she was smiling too.

At lunchtimes, one or the other of them will prepare a salad or some pasta, and they'll sit together while Annie tells Graham of progress, or setbacks, workwise, and he offers his opinion, but only when she asks for it.

"You remind me of your mum," he says to her one day.

"Do I?" Annie is pleased, not used to being compared to me. It's normally Kitty, who people say shares my optimistic, caring nature. I sometimes thought it belittled me a bit; focusing on these traditionally feminine characteristics seemed to betray my other strengths, and my successes in the workplace.

"Yes. She had the same single-mindedness as you." I feel touched at this, though it may not sound like the most flattering of descriptions.

"Did she?"

"Yes! You know she absolutely insisted on going back to work after you were born, and Kitty. It was only her being poorly that made her take a break, after Tom was born. No, your mum was very much into her job. She just didn't always show it."

Annie considers this. In her mind, as she was growing up, I was first and foremost her mum, and I am glad of that. It was how I wanted it. I arranged my shifts to suit my family, wherever I could. I did work hard, to keep both streams of my life moving but never to let my children feel second place to my work.

"I suppose she must have been," muses Annie, only now really seeing the value in my work. My career, I think. It doesn't matter now, of course, but it did then. To be treated as intelligent, my qualifications valued, even though I was often seen as 'just a nurse', all that training and medical knowledge reduced to an inferior qualification next to the all-powerful doctors. I used to tease Nick about this, though he always appreciated all of the support staff. It was one of the things that first drew me to him.

"I didn't always get it," Graham says. "Nurses get a raw deal but your mum always let me know what a difficult job it is. And you remember her reaction if anyone said 'male nurse'!"

"Or female doctor!" Annie adds, laughing. "You're right. She was a stalwart."

"She'd have loved the idea of you setting up on your own."

"Do you think?"

"Yes," Graham says, though he is not as sure as he sounds and he's right. I would have worried, seeing only the pitfalls of being a single mum with a start-up company. I'd even have thought as Graham has, that maybe Annie should have tried again with Alex. *For the sake of the baby.* What a very narrow view of the world we humans often have.

All of a sudden, something is wrong. I see Annie's face flush, then the blood drain from it, and she pushes her plate away, laying her head on her arms.

"Annie?" Graham stands, panicked.

"I'm just a bit dizzy," she says, but her words slur.

"I'm calling an ambulance," he says, immediately wishing I were there. I'd know what to do. But I am not there and now it's on him. He picks up his phone and dials 999, ignoring Annie's half-hearted protests.

"Yes, my daughter. She's pregnant... seven months... eight, maybe... she's gone faint. Her voice is slurred. I... I don't know. Annie. Annie?" He wants to shake her, just to get her back to normal, but of course knows that is not the right thing to do. Annie, can you look at me?"

She lifts her head, albeit reluctantly.

"Are you breathing OK?" Graham asks and Annie looks at him like he's stupid.

"Yes, Dad."

"No, she's not bleeding," he says. "Nothing like that. We were just having lunch then all of a sudden she's gone faint."

While an ambulance is being dispatched, the operator is asking if Annie's face is drooping. They're assessing for signs of a stroke, I know.

"Can you lift your arm, Annie?"

She does, though it annoys her.

"And the other one?"

"Yes," Annie huffs, though she's not feeling herself. She just wants to sleep. Really, really wants to sleep. Then, "I feel sick!"

She vomits across the table, splattering both her plate and Graham's.

"The ambulance is on its way," my husband says, looking in dismay at the mess, fighting his instinct to start clearing it up. "Come on love, let's get you somewhere more comfortable." He helps Annie up, relieved to see she is not too unsteady on her feet, and takes her through to the lounge, seating her on the sofa and pulling over the footstool.

"It's just a stomach bug or something," Annie grumbles, but Graham is not so sure.

"Better to get you checked over, love, it came on so suddenly."

"I've got calls this afternoon."

"I'll field them. You tell me what you need and I'll rearrange them. I'll let your brother and sister know too." He messages the family group and tries to compose a message that won't send Kitty and Tom into a tailspin, settling on the following:

No need to panic but Annie's a bit unwell. We're going to hospital just to get her checked over. I'll keep you updated.

Tom is at work at the hospital so he doesn't have his phone on him but Kitty sees the message immediately.

What can I do? Shall I come over? I can ask Meg x

No, no, don't worry, until we know what's going on. Your sister thinks it's a tummy bug.

Graham doesn't want to cause unnecessary disruption, although there is a part of him thinking what if it's something much worse and Kitty needs to come back and see her sister? In essence, he's thinking what if Annie dies? Death seems very real and realistic to him now it's happened to me. What if he's preventing Kitty from saying goodbye to her sister? And what would that mean for the baby? His imagination is going into overdrive. His heart rate is picking up, and he sits on the foot stool, shifting Annie's feet without thinking.

"Dad!" she laughs, and he's relieved to see some colour there in her cheeks. Maybe she's OK. Perhaps this is all an over-reaction… he gasps sharply at a pain in his back, and then the edges of his vision go blurry and the last thing he's aware of is the soft material of the footstool, trying its best to cushion his fall before the beautifully clean and deep pile eggshell-blue carpet rushes up to meet him and the darkness completely fills in his eyes, and the world goes black.

21

Yet again I'm watching on as my family freefall into a potential catastrophe. I see Annie's face drain again immediately as her dad tips forward onto the floor.

"Dad? Dad!" she exclaims, pushing herself forward, off the seat and onto her knees beside him, which is no mean feat.

Graham groans a little, and starts to speak. Annie can't make out the words but I know he's asking, "What am I doing down here?" His face is grey and Annie subtly takes his wrist, feeling for his pulse. Despite everything, I'm proud of her for remembering this. Annie thinks his heart is beating faster than it should, and she's right.

"Dad? Dad, I'm going to get you onto the sofa, OK?" All thoughts of her own illness have been pushed aside.

Careful, Annie, I think, wishing so much that I was able to help. I have an idea.

Graham, I whisper into my husband's ear. *You need to help Annie. You need to get onto that sofa, OK?*

He mumbles, and groans, and I think he might have

heard me or at least somehow received the message.

"Ruth?" he says.

"Mum's not here, Dad," Annie says, tears springing to her eyes. But she's made of seriously strong stuff, is Annie, and she pushes the tears and the sadness away. "Come on, let's get you up here. On the count of three…"

I count along with her. *One, two, three. Go on, Graham.*

Somehow, they do it, and now Graham is lying on the seat his daughter had previously occupied, and she is sitting on the footstool, trying to sit up straight and give her baby some space. She stretches, and stands, tentatively, finding she feels surprisingly alright. Then her lightheadedness returns, and she promptly sits down again. Her dad is conscious, though he's muttering and talking some kind of gibberish. "Ruth," he says, "1, 2, 3."

"It's OK, Dad, just keep calm and quiet. I'm going to get you a glass of water in a minute." *As long as I don't pass out when I stand up,* she thinks.

And gingerly, she stands again and finds she's OK. She's scared, though, of what is happening to her dad, and of what it would mean if she herself passed out on the way to the kitchen. What then? At least there is an ambulance on the way, she thinks, and allows herself a little laugh. They're going to be surprised to find her dad needs medical attention as well.

She makes it to the kitchen, moving slowly and keeping a hand on the wall, though she thinks she feels relatively OK. Her head is aching, but she no longer feels sick. She successfully gets a glass of water for Graham, and takes the opportunity to have a drink herself while she's at the sink, then she carries her dad's glass back to him, cursing her weakened state and wishing she was better able to help him. A movement at the front door catches her eye and makes her jump. There's a man there in high vis and behind him a woman. Annie goes to open the door.

"Hello love. My name's Rob. We're responding to a phone call made from this address…"

"Yes that was my dad. It was about me. But, it's Dad, he's… please, follow me."

A female paramedic appears at the man's shoulder. "We're here to see Anne…"

"Yes, that's me, but – you'll see. My dad's passed out, he's in here."

"I have here that your dad called about you," the woman says, though she's hurrying in behind her colleague.

"Yes, yes," Annie says impatiently, "he did. I was sick. I…"

"OK," the man says, seeing Graham, grey-faced on the sofa, assessing the scene and correctly surmising what has happened. "Can you sit down, Anne, and tell us what's happened? I'll take a look at your dad and Christine will check you over, if that's OK?"

"Yes, yes. Thank you." Annie's relief is palpable and she sits in her large chair, explaining what has happened while Christine checks her vitals. She can hear Rob talking to Graham and is pleased to hear her dad is able to talk to him relatively coherently.

Christine looks at Annie. "Your pulse is quite fast, my love."

"Your dad's too," Rob says, smiling at her. "What did you have for lunch?"

"Soup," Annie says seriously then realises he's probably joking.

"Well look, I think it's worth taking you both in to be checked over, will that be OK? Graham," he turns back to my husband, "I think you might have had some kind of heart event."

"Event?" Graham asks, his addled mind filling with an image of Badminton horse trials, which we went to one year.

"Yes, I don't know what exactly, and it may be nothing. You were obviously worried about your daughter."

"I – yes." Graham looks across the room at Annie, remembering. "Yes, I was. You were sick on the table."

"Oh dear," Rob grins. "That soup again?"

"The mess!" Annie says, moving to stand up.

Christine presses a hand to her arm. "It'll wait." She can see Annie is agitated now though. "Tell you what, I'll go and have a look, I'll sort it. OK? But I think you and your dad are both going to need seeing at the hospital – just to check you over, alright?"

"I feel much better now," says Annie.

"So do I," says Graham, but nobody believes him.

"That's as may be but you've got that little one to think about too," Christine gestures to Annie's belly, "and I'm no midwife. I won't sleep tonight if I don't know for sure you and the babe are OK. So consider this as doing me a favour, OK? And in return I'll clean up the mess in the kitchen. OK?"

"OK," says Annie, although Rob is already radioing through for a second ambulance.

"We'll take your dad first, alright? We'll get him loaded up and comfortable but we'll wait for the next ambulance so you're not left on your own."

"I'll be fine," Annie tries again, her mind turning to her laptop and the emails she's meant to be writing.

"Don't forget you're doing me a favour," Christine says sternly. "Now you sit back and we'll just see to your dad."

Christine's kindness warms Annie, making her think of the way I used to care for her. "My mum was a nurse."

"Was she?" The 'was' is not lost on Christine.

"Yes. She died, last year."

"I'm sorry, love. It's a hard thing to go through, for you and your dad. No wonder you're both out of sorts. But look, we'll have you both sorted soon. Do you need to phone anyone? Husband? Boyfriend?"

"No, nobody like that," Annie says, though she does find herself thinking of Martin and she looks forward to telling him, at the end of the day, about everything.

Once she's been given the all-clear and is back home, and hopefully Graham too. She wants to know what is happening before she contacts anyone else.

"OK, well I'll be back soon. Just sit tight, OK?"

Realising that she doesn't have much alternative without kicking up a huge fuss, Annie does as she's told, though she feels very uncomfortable seeing her dad being taken away and she leans forward to see him being walked slowly up the ramp into the back of the ambulance, leaning on Christine. A moment of panic seizes her, rushing her straight back to her childhood, and the separation anxiety she had once suffered from.

I whisper to the baby, who wakes and moves about, a jumble of limbs, reminding Annie that she is not alone and that she has in fact moved up a notch in generational terms and responsibilities. She smiles slightly and pats her belly softly. "I'm here," she whispers. "And we're OK."

And it's not long before Christine is back with her – with them – and she updates Annie on Graham. "He's OK, love. Feeling like he's making a fuss. He says he's not feeling so bad now."

"That sounds like Dad."

"It sounds like you too! I know what it's like. It's not convenient, for a start, getting whisked away in an ambulance, but it's better long-term, to make sure everything's OK."

"What do you think is wrong with Dad?"

"Oh, I don't know. I can't really say. That's what the doctors are for."

Annie knows when she is being fobbed off, but she doesn't push it. Something to do with his heart, Rob said, but she can't think of the words he used. She does feel tired, she realises, and she rests her head against the back of the seat, closing her eyes.

"Just sit tight," says Christine, "the other lot are just minutes away." And as promised she goes through to find the vomit-splattered kitchen, taking a roll of blue paper and a medical waste bag with her. She has seen a lot worse. With a large wad of paper she begins the clean-up and is incredibly quick, thorough and efficient. There's no knowing if Annie will be kept in overnight – or possibly even longer – and she doesn't want a heavily pregnant woman coming back to a mess. She places the bowls and plates in the sink and rinses them clean, then wipes down the table, chairs and floor. She disposes of all the cleaning materials and then her own gloves in the bag, sealing it shut then heading outside to put it straight in the bin. As she does so, the other ambulance pulls onto Annie's drive.

"You're certainly giving the neighbours something to talk about," Christine grins, coming in the house with two young paramedics, having given them a brief summary of the situation. "Now these two likely lads are David and Simon. I will have to leave you in their capable hands. Is that OK, Anne?"

"Yes, of course, go and make sure Dad's OK."

"Will do, love. You take care."

"I will. And thank you."

Christine gives Annie a maternal smile which makes my daughter yearn for me. But then Christine is gone and she's on her own with these two young men.

"Can you walk with me, Anne?"

"Yes," she says shortly.

"Take your time. Lean on me," Simon says. "That's what I'm here for."

And Annie finds herself wishing it was Christine she was leaning on but she does as she is told.

In his ambulance, Graham is lying on the stretcher-bed. He smiles a bit sheepishly at Christine as she climbs in.

"It sounds like you've had a tough year," she says.

Embarrassingly – to his mind – he begins to cry. "Is Annie alright?" he asks.

"She's fine. She's being well looked after and she actually seems very well. But we'll just check her over, to be on the safe side. You should be able to see her later. We'll be at the hospital in a jiffy, OK?"

Graham thinks of padded envelopes, imagining himself sliding into one like a sleeping bag. He does feel tired. "OK."

"Great." She pats his hand and they both feel the vehicle moving and then they are off, belting along the streets, Annie's ambulance hot on their tail.

22

Of course Kitty had paid no attention to Graham saying to stay put. She had a feeling that there must be more to the situation than a tummy bug, otherwise why would he have bothered to send a message? And why take Annie to hospital to get checked over if he wasn't worried?

"Annie's ill," she said bluntly, bursting through Meg's office door.

"What? Ill in what way?"

"I don't know. Dad said it's a tummy bug but I think he's worried."

"Well what are you waiting for?" Meg asked. "Go on, get over there."

"But… are you sure?"

"Of course. Gloria's in later, we'll manage. Go and see your sister and make sure she's OK. And give her my love."

"Oh thank you, Meg. I'll make it up to you."

"You already do, don't worry. If you were on flexi time I'd owe you about a year's worth of leave."

Kitty flashes her a smile though her stomach is

churning. It feels like something is very wrong, somehow, and she tries to call her dad for an update but it goes straight to voicemail. The same when she tries Tom. This is one of those times when she wishes that she hadn't moved away from home, but if she hurries she could be there in two hours, maybe less if the traffic's good.

All the way back she's on edge, and it doesn't help that she has to stop and fill up with fuel. She buys a pasty and a can of Coke to keep her going, though both just make her feel bloated and a bit disappointed. And she has Radio 4 on to keep her company but finds it very hard to concentrate on anything anyone's saying and switches to Radio 1, with its saccharine pop, the equivalent to her garage snacks. When finally she reaches the hospital, she has to drive around the car park five times, becoming increasingly agitated, and eventually lurking sharklike at the corner of one section, rewarded within a few minutes by a cheery couple who wave over to her, indicating they are about to leave. She's not taking any chances and moves the car as close to the space as she can without making it difficult for them to get out. Then she is in the space, and out of the car, and running across the car park to the maternity unit. That must be where Annie would be taken, she thinks. Or would it be A&E? No, no, she remembers a friend of hers having to be brought into hospital with gestational diabetes and she was whisked straight to the maternity section.

"Hi," she says breathlessly to the woman on reception. "I'm looking for Annie... Anne... Hebden." She is sure that Annie would have used her maiden name, and she's right.

"Ah yes, OK. And you are...?"

"Her sister."

"Lovely. She's just along the corridor there, if you take the double door second on the right and buzz through, somebody will take you to her."

The woman doesn't seem unduly concerned, but maybe that's how she has to be. Kitty tries Graham's phone again as she hurries along, trainers squeaking on the polished floor. She uses the hand-sanitiser by the double doors then presses the button and gives Annie's name, and her own, and she is allowed entrance, greeted by a woman in scrubs, who shows her along to a small bay of beds which currently only houses Annie, who is sitting up in one of those tall-backed hospital chairs, and looking remarkably well, though also quite worried.

"Annie?" Kitty says. "Oh my god, it's so good to see you. Are you OK?"

"*I* am," Annie says meaningfully.

"You're... you don't mean...?" Kitty's eyes fall to her sister's belly.

"Oh, no, sorry, the baby's OK too. We're fine."

"Your sister has raised blood pressure," a nurse says slightly sternly as she enters the room. "It sounds like she needs to do a bit less work and a bit more resting."

"Ah, well, that does sound like Annie," Kitty smiles, though she is still trying to unpick the meaning in her sister's words.

"It's Dad," Annie says more bluntly than she means to.

"What...?" Kitty looks around, realising that she had expected to see Graham there too.

"I mean, he's not well, Kitty." Annie gestures to a plain plastic chair nearby and Kitty pulls it close to Annie, sitting down, her heart pounding. Annie fills her in on what's happened. "And I'm stuck here, until they discharge me. They want to check my BP another couple of times over the next few hours, and the baby's heartbeat and all that, and they won't even let me go across and find him while I'm waiting."

"Well... no," Kitty muses. "I don't suppose you can. But I could. And Tom...?"

"He's here somewhere, working. One of the healthcare assistants is on a mission to find him so hopefully it won't be too long. Can you go and look for Dad though please, Kit? I'm worried about him."

"Of course. Do you – do you need anything?"

"No, I just want to know Dad's OK."

"Right. Well keep your phone on, if you're allowed to. I'll go and see what I can find out."

And off she goes, back out of the ward and maternity unit, scurrying across the drop-off car park then past the queue of waiting ambulances, and into the main body of the building, in the direction of A&E.

There, she sees people sitting glumly in the waiting area, and she casts a sympathetic glance at a little boy with a blood-soaked cloth held to his head by his worried mum, then joins the queue at the reception desk, trying very hard to look like she can't hear the man's very personal details he is describing to the receptionist. Eventually he is persuaded to sit back down and wait his turn, then it's a young couple who are next up, who are thankfully much more discreet than the previous man and then it is Kitty's turn.

"Hi," she smiles, sympathetic to the tough job the receptionist has. "I'm looking for my dad, Graham Hebden, he was brought in by ambulance, I don't know where he is, or anything, but I thought this would be the place to start."

"Graham...?" the woman says, her expression neither warm nor cold. Possibly years of working at the coal face have helped her develop this manner.

"Hebden," Kitty confirms.

"Ah yes, we have him here." A small smile is offered now. "He's being examined at present. Did you want to see him?"

"Yes, please," Kitty says. "Can I? May I?" she corrects herself and this wins a full smile from the woman.

"Yes, you may. I'll see if I can get somebody to take you through."

And once again Kitty is half holding her breath as she approaches a set of double doors, and she is brought through into a small unit which appears to have no daylight whatsoever, and there at the end of a row of cubicles she sees her dad's name, before she sees him, and then there he is, lying on a bed, attached to a bunch of wires and machines, but awake, and chatting to a nurse who's taking his blood pressure, and then he's smiling to see his younger daughter.

"Kitty! What are you doing here?" He goes to sit up and the nurse puts a gentle hand on his shoulder.

"Try and keep still. And calm," she says, mock-sternly.

"Sorry, I'll do my best. This is my daughter though."

"I see." The nurse surreptitiously scans Kitty.

"My younger daughter," Graham clarifies. "Not the pregnant one."

"Ah, I see. That makes sense!" The nurse smiles at Kitty. "I'll be out of your way in a minute, and you can sit down."

"Thank you. But can you tell me what's going on? Dad? I came in to see Annie, and she sent me over here."

"Is Annie alright? And the baby?"

"Yes, they're both fine. She says it's high blood pressure. She's been working too hard, probably. But what about you?"

"I had, probably – they think – maybe a heart event?" Graham looks at the nurse like a young boy asking his mother something. It squeezes at Kitty's own heart, to see him look so vulnerable.

"Yes, we think so. We're doing lots of tests, don't worry," the nurse addresses Kitty. "But we don't think it was a full heart attack."

"Oh, OK," Kitty says, having no idea how any of this works. "So what does that mean? Can he come home?"

"That's up to the doctors but I think they'll want to keep him in overnight, just to make sure." Graham's face falls. The nurse laughs. "It's OK, we're not so bad. And we'll move you onto a ward if there's space. Somewhere with actual windows!"

Kitty looks around her, thinking it must be hard working in a place like this. It feels almost like she imagines a spaceship might.

"I'd like to go home if I can," Graham says in a small voice.

"I know, I understand, but your blood pressure's still up," the nurse pats his shoulder then expertly removes the sleeve that's been around his upper arm. "Just rest up, and try and get some sleep if you can. You'll be home again before you know it. And on grandad duties too before too long, by the sound of things!"

"Well, yes…" Graham looks pleased at the thought of this and as the nurse moves out, Kitty shuffles along and sits down next to the bed.

"What happened, Dad?"

Graham relays as much of the afternoon's events as he can remember. "But Annie and the baby are definitely fine?" he asks.

"They are, Dad, they are." Kitty pats his hand, then feels her phone vibrate. She pulls it from her pocket. "It's Tom! Hello," she says to her brother, "are you OK?"

"I'm fine," he says, "but I've just seen Dad's message, and he's not answering."

"No, that's because he's at the hospital. Listen, he's actually been brought in himself." She holds her hand up and smiles at Graham as he tries to insist that he is absolutely fine.

"I thought he said Annie was ill?"

"She is, well she's OK, but they're both here. Annie at maternity and Dad in A&E."

"What?"

"Yeah. Are you working? Can you get down to see us? I'm with Dad at the moment."

"I'll be right there."

So Tom, who was close to the end of his shift anyway, clears it with his manager and hotfoots it down to the A&E department, quickly finding Graham and earning sympathetic looks from those colleagues who know him. He is pretty much universally liked, is Tom, though I'm not sure he quite appreciates that.

"There you are!" he says, bursting into Graham's cubicle. "Are you alright, Dad?"

"All the better for seeing you, son. But now you're both here, can one of you go and see Annie please?"

"I'll go," says Kitty. "You can fill Tom in on what's

going on. But let me know if you get moved onto a ward please."

And she vacates her seat so Tom can fill it and with slower steps than before she retraces her path across to the maternity unit, and gets buzzed back through to see Annie, who is still sitting up, right as rain, and itching to get back home and to her laptop but being forced to wait instead, and watch daytime TV, which she tells Kitty will make her blood pressure go through the roof. Sensibly, Kitty switches off the TV and then tells Annie what she has learned about Graham and the two of them Google 'heart event' and learn that it is unlikely to have been brought on by stress, and that Graham might well have some underlying cardiac issues.

"So I guess I did him a favour by being sick," Annie smiles and Kitty grins at her, delighted by her sister's unexpected good humour. What she doesn't know is that since she first came to see her, Annie has been exchanging messages with Martin, whose evident concern and kindness is making Annie feel unexpectedly wonderful.

"I guess you did. Very kind of you. But maybe you do need to slow down," Kitty suggests.

"Yes, I think that would be a good idea." A voice startles them, and they look round to see Alex, who by chance had called round to see Annie, to find his old neighbour, Roger, rushing across to update him on events. All Alex knows is that Annie was carried off in an ambulance. Nobody has yet thought to tell him what happened or where she is.

"Alex!" Kitty says, standing to greet him. She finds herself hugging him, and sees how worried he looks, and she feels bad that she didn't think to tell him what was happening. Annie, too, looks a little shamefaced, particularly as she thinks she's been keeping Martin, a relative stranger, updated on events.

"I was going to call you," she says, "when I knew what was happening."

"Don't you think I'd have wanted to know anyway?" he asks, but he is trying not to be annoyed or make Annie feel worse. "What's going on, Annie?"

"I'll leave you to it," says Kitty, and she stands to make space for Alex, leaving him and Annie to talk and once more trekking across the hospital grounds but stopping this time for a little while, to calm her own breathing down and just take stock of everything. She sits at a picnic table on top of a small grassy mound, and watches the other people moving around her: drivers circling as she had done, increasingly desperate for a parking space; an older couple moving slowly back towards their own car; a young man on crutches; a family with three kids. She wonders what is happening with all of them and she wishes them well, and she considers how rarely she had been to this hospital before the last eighteen months, and then how much a part of her life it had become.

Since my diagnosis, and her bringing me to a couple

of appointments, and visiting me when I'd been admitted with a high temperature while I was undergoing chemo, and various other check-ups and appointments until it was clear they could do no more for me here, this place has become all too familiar. They were back here when Tom had his accident and now here they are again. She's the only one of us, in fact, who hasn't been admitted here. She sighs, knowing now is not the time for such contemplation, then she stands and heads back into A&E, to find her dad and brother. A grey-haired man with a name badge that indicates he works at the hospital stands back to let her through.

"Thank you," she smiles at him.

"No problem," says Nick, and smiles back.

23

"So are you going to let me in on what's happening?" Alex asks and he can't help feeling a bit like he's in a TV show. That sounds like the kind of question a straight-talking, no-nonsense kind of character might say. And that is how he wants to present himself now. With Donna's support he's built up a bit of a froth over how left out he has been when it comes to his estranged wife and his in utero baby. To be quite honest, I don't blame him.

Annie looks at him and rolls her very tired eyes, raising one of her brows at Alex's tone of voice.

But, "No, don't look at me like that, Annie–" all thoughts of TV and an imaginary audience forgotten, Alex lets forth – "with that patronising expression. I've had enough of it. I'm not an idiot, or a child. I'm your – well, I'm still actually your husband, legally, though I know that doesn't count for much, but I am the father of that baby, and that counts for a lot. I've barely seen you lately, and I don't mean in a husband-and-wife type way but I really need to have some kind of involvement with this pregnancy. And yes, I know, it's your pregnancy, your body. I wouldn't dream of saying otherwise. You know I'm not like that. But I would like to have some kind of update, just to know everything's OK – or not. I mean, *are* you OK? And the baby?"

Alex knows Annie much better than she gives him credit for. He's pre-empted any objection she might make and he's said so much more in that little speech than he has in a long time. He stops, almost breathless, and tries not to feel slightly elated that he has finally spoken up for himself, properly. Donna would be proud, he thinks, and pushes away the thought that his mum would be too.

"I'm sorry Alex," Annie sighs. She rubs her eyes, then looks at him and it feels like she is seeing him properly for the first time in years. Before her is a man she knows so well; like nobody else, in fact. And she looks at that familiar face, really looks at it, seeing the same wide mouth, and the slightly crooked nose, and those kind eyes, and she realises that over the years this man, this face, had become incidental to her life. Even if she had been sitting across the table from him, she wouldn't have been looking at him properly. And right now, a little part of her thinks she misses him.

For Alex's part, it's all he can do to prevent himself from immediately telling her it's OK, trying to comfort her. But no, it's not OK. He hears Donna's voice telling him that and he's grateful to her. For listening to him, and actually hearing him, and telling him he has rights too. He remembers the Anonymous movement, those men scaling Big Ben, protesting for their rights to be involved in their children's lives. It would never come to that with Annie, he is sure, though maybe some of those men thought that too. Then again, maybe some of those men were kept out of their children's lives with good reason. Perhaps some of them may have been bullies and that was just another way for them to try to control 'their' women and children. It's impossible to know, but what Alex does know is that he would never try to control Annie. He couldn't. He just wants to be involved, and to have a say, in their child's life.

"Our marriage might be over, Annie, but we're still family, aren't we? I mean, all of a sudden I've lost not just you but your whole family. Graham, Tom… Kitty," he says tentatively, looking for a reaction.

"But you've got your mum and dad," Annie says, black and white as ever.

"Yes, but I've been a part of your family for years, you know, or at least I felt like it. I saw Tom grow up, I was there when Ruth was ill. I'm – they're so important to me. Just because you and I aren't together anymore doesn't mean that just stops. And the – our – baby. Oh my god Annie, I can't tell you how excited I am about it."

"Are you?"

"Yes!" he exclaims, eyes shining. "So, so excited! And you know, I want you to know I will be there, at the birth if you want me to or, no, maybe not the birth? It's up to you. But I'll be waiting outside, ready if you need me and waiting to see our little boy or girl. I – it is OK, isn't it? I mean, you look OK…"

"It's fine, Alex." Annie actually smiles at him. "The baby is fine and I'm fine. I just have a bit of high blood pressure."

"OK, OK, so is it time to go on maternity leave?"

Annie looks at him, seeing how much she has kept from him. Not deliberately or maliciously but just from not having seen a reason to tell him. "About that…"

Alex listens as Annie tells him what's been happening in her life, with her work, and her fledgling business.

"So you're going independent?" Alex asks, looking at her with wide eyes.

"Yes." Annie waits for similar objections to Graham's.

"That is amazing! I never thought they appreciated you enough. Overworked and underpaid, I always thought."

"Really?"

"Yes, really."

Annie is smiling widely at this man in front of her, a froth of fondness washing at the edges of her mind. "I thought you'd think it was a terrible idea. Lack of security and all that… a baby on the way, no steady income…"

"But Annie, that's what I'm trying to tell you. You're not on your own in this. The baby is both of our responsibilities. And I may not have the highest paid job in the world but you know it's alright, and financially this child is both of our responsibilities. And I want to be involved practically too. You know that. We can work it out. You could be more flexible in your hours than me so I can have the baby in the evenings – at your house if you like – while you get things done. Or I can ask at work about compressing my week. You know they're getting better about those things…"

His enthusiasm is so touching, and Annie is so tired, she feels tears welling up; far more regular visitors these days than she's ever been used to. Even our Annie is not immune to the effects of hormones. But also, these little shining drops of moisture are a genuine reaction to this lovely man. Because when all is said and done, that's what Alex is.

"Our baby is very lucky to have you," Annie says, unusually generous in her sentiments. "And so am I."

So unused to compliments from Annie, Alex has to look at her to check she's being serious, but her face tells him that she is.

"So where are they, anyway?"

"Where are who?" Annie is confused.

"The rest of the Hebdens! I mean, I know Kitty was here but where are Graham and Tom?"

"Oh, God, I haven't told you. Dad's here too."

"Where?" Alex looks around, confused.

"In hospital. He had – a 'heart event', they're calling it. It's not a heart attack, I don't think. Or not a cardiac arrest. I don't know. Kitty and I were trying to educate ourselves about it."

"Is he alright though?" Alex thinks of his father-in-law, and a memory of me flits through his mind too, rapidly bringing thoughts of my illness and death, and he hopes that Annie is not about to lose her other parent. He hopes he is not about to lose his other parent-in-law, even if it's felt like Graham is only tolerating Alex at times.

"I think so. I mean, you could go and see him, if you want to."

"I don't know. Would he want me to?"

"I – maybe." Annie smiles.

"I'll maybe leave it to Kitty and Tom. Graham will probably want his privacy."

"Yes, maybe you're right."

"I need to get home anyway, Mum's doing tea."

"Of course." But she doesn't mean it in a bad way. "Send her my love, will you? And your dad."

"I will." Alex stands and places a kiss on Annie's forehead. "Take care, and keep in touch, OK? Properly, I mean."

"I will. I promise. And Alex?"

"Yes?"

"Thank you."

Annie is allowed home, with strict instructions to rest regularly and to contact her midwife or the hospital at the first sign of any adverse physical changes.

"I have to exercise too," she tells Graham when she visits him on the ward he's been moved to before she heads home. "Just walking. Maybe some swimming."

"I'll join you!" he volunteers.

"That would be nice. I think Alex is going to take me swimming though."

"Oh?" Graham raises his eyebrows.

"Nothing like that. He's just – he's part of our lives, isn't he? And he always will be. And he will be a good dad," she says firmly.

"I don't doubt it," says Graham. "He's a good lad really. Just not right for you."

"No. Anyway, you look tired, Dad. Get some rest."

"And you too love. I'll get those jobs done, when I'm back. Don't worry. We'll have everything right before the baby comes."

"We will," Annie says, thinking there's no way she's going to let Graham do any more than mow the lawn for her. Not till he's been given the all-clear. But she will let him down gently when he's back home. "Goodnight, Dad," she says.

"Night, Annie." His shoulders seem to relax and he sinks into his bed a little. "What a day, eh?" he murmurs.

"You can say that again."

"What a day, eh?" He manages a sleepy smile.

Kitty and Tom are waiting for Annie outside and Kitty drives the three of them back to Annie's. It feels strange, walking into the house, and like it's been days since she was last there, rather than hours. The kitchen is, she is very pleased to note, free of any sign of her sickness, and she casts her mind gratefully back to Christine, then wonders what else those paramedics have had to deal with today, after her and Graham. The two of them were probably a relatively easy job, she thinks, and I'm proud of Annie for thinking like this. It seems like she is increasingly more engaged these days, considering other people's situations and even – dare I say it? – feelings.

Kitty says she will stay overnight and Annie doesn't protest, though she is not worried for herself.

"I'll get back to Mavis," Tom says, though his sisters know it's Cecily he's keen to return to as well. She has been dog-sitting since Tom rang and told her what was happening, realising that Mavis had already been on her own for hours. In fact, our beloved dog has slept pretty much all the time Cecily's been with her but at least she knows she is not alone.

It's another three days before Graham is allowed back home and he's so glad to be away from the ward and

236

the shouting of the poor man in the bed opposite, who is suffering from dementia and not at all happy with the tubes that are attached to him.

Graham has a new lot of medication to get started on, and a range of appointments to go back for various tests and consultations, but he feels OK. Much better now he is home. And he's starting to feel like he should get back to his list of tasks at Annie's, as that baby's not going to wait.

As it turns out, though, Alex has picked up where Graham has left off and Annie tells her dad in no uncertain terms that he is not to feel aggrieved at this.

"Alex wants to help. And don't forget, Dad, this is – or was – his house too, even though he no longer lives here. We have to sort that out at some point but Alex has a stake in this place, and this baby. This is his house. His baby." She hammers the point home and Graham has to take it.

Alex too has been having some words with his parents, who want to know why he's putting himself out to help the woman who to their minds just dropped him 'like a hot potato' as Celia puts it.

"That's not how it is," Alex tells her, though he still stops short of detailing how it actually is. What actually happened between him and Kitty.

"Well I say she's using you, Alex."

"She is not!" he exclaims angrily. "I offered to do all this. I want to. She's still my – well, she's the woman I married, and the mother of my child. And I still love her, and care about her. And the others. They are my family too, they always will be."

"She won't let you have a look-in when the baby comes."

"She will, Mum," Alex says. "And you too." He knows that's what bothers her really. She has longed to be a grandmother and now it's happening she thinks Annie will keep her out.

"She'd better," Celia huffs.

"Really, she will. But you need to respect her."

"I beg your pardon?"

"You need to respect Annie, and how she wants to be a mother. It might be different to what you would do, but this is her baby. Her time to be a mum. You need to respect that and honestly Mum, the more you do, the more welcome you will be."

"Oh, so I'm not welcome if I don't like something?"

"That's not what I'm saying, Mum. But you – well, you do like to tell people what you think is best."

"I don't!" Celia is outraged. Behind his newspaper, her husband coughs. She whirls round to face him. "What?"

"Listen to Alex, my love. He's right. This is Annie's baby – and his. And our grandchild, yes, but we have to step back. Unless there is something really wrong – and there won't be, because Annie and Alex will be excellent parents – then we stand back and we step in when we are needed and when we are wanted."

Alex is slightly stunned by his dad's words, but he

sees his mum is floundering now, all at sea in the middle of her front room, and he feels a rush of sympathy for her, and he steps forward, this dad-to-be, and puts his arms around her.

"You don't need to tell anyone else how to be a mum," he says. "You're already the best."

24

It feels to Annie as though all of a sudden the midwife appointments have picked up pace, and there are antenatal classes which she really wouldn't have bothered with, only Alex has said that he thinks they should go, and he's amazed at how easily she capitulates.

"Donna says her sister made a really lovely group of friends at their classes, and they're still getting together now, and the children are nearly school age."

It would seem that despite their years of marriage and their renewed closeness, Alex is still able to miss the mark when it comes to Annie. The thought of having to become part of a group of friends whose only common ground is having children the same age is not something she relishes. But she is finding her feelings towards Alex these days are so different, and she's so grateful to him for his help and support – and fond of him, too. Should she be fond? Is that a terrible way to think of her ex-husband? But it's the word that springs to mind.

She thinks often of what he said in the hospital, of how he's felt like he's lost her whole family in splitting up with her, and Annie can actually understand that. She doesn't feel the same about his parents; they have never been close, but Alex has been a part of our world for a long time, in and out of our house ever since he and Annie got together.

He hasn't told Annie about the words he's had with his mum, but he does drop his parents into conversation quite regularly. He's working up to asking about their involvement when the baby's here, but he's still not quite there yet. Instead, he and Annie are working on a plan to have regular times and days.

"It will be easier when you're not breastfeeding anymore," he says.

Annie's head shoots up from the paper she'd been reading.

"You are going to do that, aren't you?" One of their antenatal classes has been about the benefits of breastfeeding.

"I – don't know." Annie thinks guiltily of the bottles and tins of formula she has secreted in her own wardrobe. There's a part of her that just can't get her head around breastfeeding and she worries how she might feel about it.

"OK," Alex is wise enough not to push it, "well just say you do, you might be able to pump some milk so I can do some feeds, but the health visitor did say that can be difficult. So – it would be difficult, I guess, to leave him or her with me for too long. But I can be here, and on hand, or Graham can, or…" He wants to say his mum could help but he holds back on that as well. "But you do need to look after yourself too, you know. I realise you're starting a business but I, well it's a big deal for you. Pregnancy puts a lot of strain on your body, and it seems like having a baby is pretty full-on. You do need to look after yourself, for your sake and for all our sakes."

He's worried about Annie just ploughing straight back into her work once she and the baby are home. He has listened very well at antenatal classes, and sees how all-consuming a new baby will be. He's just not sure Annie does.

"I will." She pats his hand.

"Don't do that!"

"What?"

"The hand thing. I'm not a child, you know. I can't just be fobbed off with a couple of comforting words. I really mean it, you need to look after yourself. You've already got high blood pressure."

It's getting higher right now, she thinks. And she is grateful for her phone pinging.

It's on the table in front of her and they both instinctively look at the screen.

"Who's Martin?" Alex asks.

"Who? Oh, erm, just a work contact."

It does not escape Alex's attention that Annie looks like she is squirming a little. "Really?"

"Yes, really," she snaps.

"Are you sure?"

"Yes, I'm sure, Alex. And even if he wasn't, what's it to you?"

"What it is to me, Annie–" he finds himself taken aback at how quickly enraged he feels but he is powerless to stop it – "is that you're about to have my baby. We're trying to build a world where we can both care for him or her, and maybe our – our families – can have a role too. So that you can keep working, I might add. And I don't think it's right to be introducing some – some stranger – to the set-up. In fact I don't feel comfortable about some strange bloke being around my child."

"And is Donna going to be allowed access?" Annie asks coldly.

"Is she —? I. I don't know. I hadn't thought about it." In fact, Donna has been a bit put out by Alex's absence these last few weeks, although she's being a brick, as Celia puts it.

"Maybe I don't want some strange woman around my child," Annie suggests.

"That's different."

"Why?"

"Because – because she's a woman."

"I don't think that argument holds a lot of weight, Alex. What is it about being a woman that makes her so qualified for being around a baby? And why should I feel comfortable with it?"

"You know what I mean, Annie. And anyway, how have you had time to meet a new man?" This is the crux of the matter. Alex is jealous. He's been enjoying his role looking after Annie, and her actually letting him. And he's got the best of both worlds, with Donna there for him, supporting him; admiring him, even, and wanting to spend time with him. He never felt that Annie was bothered if he was around or not. Donna, on the other hand, seems to be looking forward to having more time with him, once the baby's born.

He has felt like a bit of a hero, if he's honest. Gallantly supporting his ex-wife, and taking that male role in her life that she clearly needs. Now he feels threatened. What if this Martin bloke steps up, wants to be involved? Wants to move in? Images tumble into his mind of a future where Annie remarries, and he, Alex, is sidelined, an afterthought in his child's life. Well he won't have it.

"Alex," Annie says impressively calmly, "it's none of your business."

"Of course it's my business!" he snaps. "If you can't see that, then, well, I don't know." He stands abruptly. "I'm going out." He needs some space and he knows he shouldn't be upsetting Annie this way.

"Fine. Good idea." Annie takes their mugs to the sink, tipping away the remains of Alex's drink and watching it gurgle down the plughole as the front door slams. "What a prick," she says to herself, though she covers her tummy with one hand so the baby won't hear.

Then she thinks, *It's not moving. It hasn't moved for ages. When did it last move?* She begins to panic. Breathes slowly. Tries to calm herself down. Did it wake her with a sharp kick this morning – or was that yesterday? The days have begun to blur a little.

Annie goes back to her phone, swiping Martin's message clear and calling Alex immediately. It goes straight to voicemail. She phones his parents' house, hopes for his dad. Damn.

"Hi Celia, it's Anne."

"Oh hello," Celia's voice is thin and reedy, never having been quite sure how to speak naturally to her daughter-in-law.

"Is Alex there? Well, no, he won't be yet, I don't suppose. He's just left here. But I can't get through to him. Could you ask me to call me, when he's back?" She just hopes he is heading straight to his parents' home, he will be there in minutes.

"I will. Is everything OK?" Celia asks cautiously. She is, if she is very honest, a bit afraid of her soon to be ex-daughter-in-law. Annie is so intelligent and educated to Celia's mind – and it's true, she is, but Celia thinks that makes her haughty. What she's missing is how unsure of herself Annie is. How scared of social interaction and how sure she is that people don't like her. It makes her prickly and defensive, exacerbating the problem.

"Yes, fine," Annie says breezily. "If you can get Alex to call me though please, Celia."

And she puts the phone down!

Annie! I think. *No wonder Celia thinks you're haughty.*

"You're right. Sorry, Mum," Annie says, shocking me. Has she heard me? No, I realise, she has just happened to see a picture she has of me on her shelf, and in doing so thought what I would have advised if I'd been there. Which of course I am, she just doesn't know it. Annie unlocks her phone, dials the same number again.

"Celia?" she says before her mother-in-law has even said hello. "It's Anne again."

"Oh, well…" Alex's mum is tempted to give her a piece of her mind, but something stops her and it's not just the fear of what Annie might say back. "What is it?" she asks more softly.

"It's… probably nothing, but the baby… it hasn't moved. For hours. Or at least I don't think it has. I'm not sure. It's… oh never mind, I'm probably worrying over nothing."

"Sit tight Anne, I'm coming over."

"You don't have to…"

"No, I'm coming. I'll whip you over to the hospital to get checked out. And I am sure you're right, it's probably nothing. But better to be sure."

"Oh, thank you Celia. Are you sure…?"

"I am more than sure. I'm on my way."

Annie sinks onto the chair, surprisingly relieved and grateful. She could have phoned Graham of course but she's ever aware of the precarious state of his health. Would a worry about the baby provoke another heart 'event'?

Kitty and Tom will both be working and Annie thinks she has been disruptive enough to their lives of late. And this will almost certainly turn out to be nothing, and she'll have worried everyone for no reason. She gets to her feet and finds her bag, letting herself out of the front door and locking up behind her, ready for Celia who, true to her word, arrives within minutes. She pulls up, gets out of the car and hugs Annie, giving her a quick once-over. The hug was unexpected for both of them. But Annie finds she is glad of it.

"No sign of Alex?" she asks once she's settled in the passenger seat, gently pulling her seatbelt over and under her bump.

"No, did he say he was heading home?" Celia restarts the car and begins to reverse out of the drive. She is meticulously careful in this as she is in all her actions. Annie can smell her floral-scented perfume and it's comforting. She considers how Alex said he misses her family. Not once has she thought she missed his, but now, in this car, with this woman who she really has known for a large part of her life, Annie realises that actually perhaps she has missed her. Just a little bit. It's just that missing me takes precedence.

Celia is a stickler for speed limits but she does go at the very top end of each, to get her daughter-in-law and unborn grandchild to the hospital as quickly as she can. As they drive, she asks Annie questions, at first about whether she's sure about the lack of movement, and then about the new business, trying to take both their minds off their worries and also trying her best to understand this woman a bit better.

It takes twenty-five minutes to get to the hospital and Celia drops Annie right outside the maternity unit, then heads off to find a parking space. "Go in!" she says. "Don't wait for me."

I wasn't going to, thinks Annie, but out loud says, "Thank you Celia."

She walks into the increasingly familiar building and goes to the reception desk where she explains what's been happening. "I know I should have called the midwife first but it's after hours. And I didn't want to go to A&E…"

"No, I don't blame you," the woman says sympathetically, eyeing up Annie's sizeable tummy. "I'll call through and get somebody to come out to you, OK love? You just sit down."

Within a couple of minutes, Annie is being guided through the sets of doors and right back to the assessment bay that she had been in just weeks before. "Somebody will be right with you," the healthcare assistant says. "Can I just take some details please?"

Annie explains that she hasn't felt the baby moving and as she takes in her surroundings and considers how many people have been through here before her, and what situations have occurred, she remembers somebody – maybe the midwife in the antenatal classes – that pregnancies are not always straightforward, and she feels a bit clammy and worried and then she feels sick, and just like in the kitchen with Graham that day, before she is able to do anything about it, she is vomiting, all over herself and the bed she is sitting on.

The young woman with her rushes to the door and spies a colleague – an older, competent midwife, and calls her in, and soon Annie has a blood pressure cuff on her arm, and she's being told that they are going to carry out a non-stress test on her baby, and they need to take her to another room for this, and she's being shifted onto a trolley and sped away to a different room, where the healthcare assistant – Gemma, she says her name is - stays by her side, cleaning her up as best she can while the original midwife begins to apply gel to Annie's tummy then explains she is doing some tests to check the baby's heartbeat and movement, using ultrasound and tocodynamometer transducers, and it's all very safe and shouldn't cause the baby any harm.

A second woman comes in, and they watch the screen with a graph that means very little to Annie, and I stay close to her, feeling the chill of fear which has lain over her like a morning frost, and only solidifies as she tries to read the women's expressions. It is not difficult, even for Annie – not the most empathic of people – to see that there is some concern there.

"What is it?" she asks. "You can tell me."

"Baby's heart rate has dropped a little," says the first midwife. "It's probably nothing to worry about, but I think we should do an ultrasound, see what's going on in there."

"OK," Annie says slowly, that frost turning to ice. "Can you do that now? Here?"

"We need an ultrasound technician, but I know she's nearby. Hold tight and we'll whip you over to the scan room, and meet her there." The second midwife leaves to arrange this, and Annie is once more wheeled into the corridor, and through a different set of double doors, then another. She keeps her hands on her belly, lying rigidly on the trolley.

"Anne!" she hears. "Annie!"

"Celia!" Annie exclaims, and she's never been so glad to see her mother-in-law. "Oh Celia," and she starts sobbing, and Alex's mum's face falls.

"It's the baby. Its heartbeat... its heart..."

The midwife takes over, asking who Celia is, checking if Annie is happy to have her with her and, Annie is amazed to find, yes she is, and explaining the situation in a calm, clear way. They move through another set of doors and into a room where, true to her word, the second midwife is, with another woman, who introduces herself as the sonographer. She wastes no time in wiping Annie's poor swollen belly clean of any remnants of gel, only to apply a whole new layer, and she begins to press the handset firmly but not uncomfortably on Annie's abdomen. It is not lost on Annie or Celia that the screen is turned discreetly away from them, and while Gemma stays with Annie, the two midwifes watch the screen intently, along with the sonographer, who is so practised it seems she barely needs to look at Annie herself.

"Mm-hmm," says midwife number one. "Alright Anne, I think I can see what the problem is."

"So there is a problem?" Celia asks, slightly shrilly, and the midwife shoots her a look.

"It looks to me like Baby's umbilical cord has become wrapped round its neck. It's called a nuchal cord, and it's very common, and not as terrifying as it sounds. But I do think we need to do something, especially given your blood pressure."

"Alright," Annie says, slightly reassured by this but not entirely convinced that she isn't being duped. "So what is the something we need to do?"

"I need to speak to the consultant and discuss with her the best course of action. And you will be consulted, I promise. I just need to make sure that we're in agreement first."

"But what would the course of action be?" Annie presses.

"There are a number of options. We need to choose the one that is best for you and Baby."

"And what's most likely?" Annie is not giving up.

"Well, like I say, I need to speak to our consultant, but I think a C-section may be an option."

"A caesarean?" Annie asks, of course well versed in all potential methods of giving birth and the pros and cons. "But couldn't that make my blood pressure worse?"

"That can be a side effect, yes. But look, let me get the doctor and she can discuss it all with you, and we'll take it from there."

"Alright," Annie agrees reluctantly.

When the midwife leaves, Celia sinks into the chair by Annie's bed. She looks pale.

"We'll be alright, Celia," Annie says. It makes me smile. "But can you maybe try Alex again?"

"Oh, of course…" Celia fishes her phone out of her bag.

"Maybe outside would be better? You know, with all these medical instruments around," Annie suggests.

"Yes, yes, I'll be as quick as I can," says Celia, and she scurries off, into a web of corridors that all look the same. It takes her a little while to get outside. Which Annie was counting on, because by the time Celia has returned – having still not been able to speak to her son, but having filled in her husband on what's happening – everything has been agreed and Annie is being prepped for an operation. Her baby is about to be delivered to her, from the other side of a blue screen, and she is about to be anaesthetised so that she will feel nothing – or she very much hopes that will be the case.

Take a deep breath, Annie, she tells herself, as she knows that is what I'd be saying.

Take a deep breath, Annie, I echo, though I know she can't hear me.

"Can you come with me, Celia?" she asks, and her mother-in-law is beside herself.

"Me? Really? Are you sure?"

"Yes," Annie says through gritted teeth. "Really. I need you."

Remember this moment, Celia thinks, and she squeezes Annie's hand.

Annie tries to smile, though her teeth are chattering with nerves. Once more wheeled again through the hospital corridors, she is taken to the operating theatre, and she's beginning to feel a bit strange, almost dreamlike. They pass a porter pushing a patient in a wheelchair and Annie thinks at first that it's Tom, then she thinks it's Sam, the doorman from her office, but then she can't think of anything but this baby, and Celia's hand in hers, and the baby – the baby.

Please Mum, can you help us? she asks, though I know she doesn't really believe I'm still around. But she will try anything.

"OK, Anne. Are you ready?" she is asked by the lovely doctor, now scrubbed up and hiding behind a mask.

Annie nods, knowing there is no going back. She is as ready as she will ever be.

25

Annie is moving restlessly in her sleep, dreaming again of me, and food.

"Olive?" I ask my dream daughter, passing a small bowl of them across the table. She and I are sitting once more under the shade of a pergola, on an Italian hillside. Tuscany, I'm sure of it. The hills are lined with vineyards and the day is almost unbearably hot. But Annie is relaxed, and for some reason relieved. "Yes," she says, accepting my offering. "Thanks, Mum."

She opens her eyes, awake in a finger-click, and it's like waking into another dream. There in a see-through cot beside her bed is her daughter. Wrapped and cosy, a soft, lemon-yellow hat on her head and her eyes squeezed shut as though she is having to concentrate on this sleeping lark.

"Olive," Annie muses, her recent dream memory still just in reach. "Yes," she says again – and then again, "Thanks, Mum."

She is alone in her cubicle – except she's not. She is with her daughter. This is the way it's going to be from now on, she thinks, and experiences a delicious thrill at the thought.

Never in her wildest dreams had she imagined she would be a maternal type but already the strength of her love for this unbelievably small and vulnerable human, with her dark blue eyes and tiny, surprisingly wrinkly, fingers and toes, is overwhelming. This has fed that relief she was feeling while she was asleep as in the darkest, furthers corners of Annie's mind she had been convinced that she would be prone to post-natal depression. That it would fit her character perfectly. Of course it doesn't work like that, and Annie is fully aware of the fact, but it was a fear nevertheless, and fear is often illogical.

It had been a tense time in the operating room while Annie and Celia waited for the confirming, soul-lifting sound of the baby's cry. And it probably took only a few seconds but they stretched out like the marks which had finally made an appearance on Annie's belly in these last few weeks of pregnancy.

For my daughter, that cry brought relief and joy and tears, and it marked another beginning. For me, it marked an ending as my granddaughter slipped fully from this world into that, and I feel her absence, just as Annie feels slightly off-balance without the weight of a baby in her belly.

But I am delighted. Elated. Over the moon. Seeing my girl, with her girl. Olive. It's a perfect name.

And Annie sits up now, gingerly, sorely. She is wearing compression stockings to reduce the risk of a blood clot, and she has a dressing on her wound, and she feels like a mess, but she doesn't care. She has eyes only for her baby, and her baby is perfect.

She can hear other babies crying elsewhere on the ward, and she wishes she was at home, though she is also grateful for the safety net of the hospital. While she is here she wants to learn to feed Olive properly, and bathe her safely, and interrogate the midwives about what to expect, and development hurdles, and…

Hush, Annie, I sweep a hand across her forehead. *All of that will come…*

And she leans back against the raised-up bed, her pristine pillow, and sighs. Then she marvels that she has not thought about work for hours. Until now. But she finds she is able to push it away, and instead she relives the last few hours.

Celia had been by her side throughout and when they'd heard that cry she had hugged Annie, tears in her eyes. "I'm so proud of you," she surprised herself by saying, and Annie surprised herself by how much those words moved her.

And they brought the baby to Annie, and Celia took photos, and then all of a sudden Alex was there, scrubbed up and face-masked and overflowing with tears.

"Here," Annie said, smiling with a rush of maternal love that extended to her ex-husband. "Here she is, Alex. And she's perfect."

Celia, herself overcome at the sight of her son meeting his baby for the first time, stepped back and away, and sank gratefully into one of the seats in the corridor, feeling silent tears rolling freely down her cheeks, dripping onto her legs and creating tiny wet marks on her chinos.

"Like this?" Alex said, trying to control his shaking as the midwife delivered his baby from Annie's chest to his arms.

"Yes," she smiled. "She's a beauty."

"My god, she is," Alex breathed, gazing down into the biggest, bluest, most beautiful eyes he had ever seen in his life. His baby gazed back.

The midwife took photos on Annie's phone. "Would you like some family shots too?" she smiled.

Alex looked doubtfully towards Annie.

"Yes please," she smiled. "If you can help me sit up a bit better."

When Alex was standing next to her, still holding his baby as though she was the most precious thing on Earth – which, of course to him she is – Annie said, "We are a family, Alex. We always will be. No matter what. You, me and her."

He leaned forward carefully and kissed Annie's forehead tenderly. It made for a beautiful photo.

Later, in the recovery room, Graham, Kitty and Tom had come in, while Annie had been drifting in and out of sleep. Alex's dad, James, had already been in, accompanied by Celia, who was trying very hard not to feel smug that they had met their granddaughter before Annie's family had.

"Annie was incredible," she told her husband. "So calm, and brave. Honestly. This little girl has a wonderful role model."

A more cynical person might suggest she could have been trying to curry favour with Annie, her eyes on the prize of having her granddaughter to herself one day a week. She has whispered this offer to Alex already, when Annie was talking to the midwife, and she's not going to let it drop. Surely now she has been so instrumental in the baby's birth, Annie will let her have more of a role in her life. And besides, it's Alex's decision too. "We'll work it out, Mum," he said.

And that more cynical person might also see, correctly, that I am just a bit jealous of Celia. That she will, undoubtedly, have a role in this little girl's life, while I will be a name, and no doubt the subject of many stories as my family try to bring me to life for my granddaughter, but at the end of the day I will be little more than an image in so many photographs. And I can't deny that is hard.

There were hugs and words of congratulations exchanged when Graham, Kitty and Tom arrived.

"She's beautiful," Celia had said, unable to help

herself asserting a tiny bit of ownership.

"Thank you for being there," Graham said, taking her hands in his. "Really."

"It was my pleasure," she replied, wrong-footed by his genuineness. "I wouldn't have had it any other way."

After more hugs and congratulations, Alex offered to walk to his parents' car with them. "Annie's asleep at the moment. And the baby," he whispered. "But go on in. The midwives will keep popping in too, Annie's got to be monitored for a while. She's been through a lot."

And Graham, tears brimming at his eyelids, walked in just ahead of Tom and Kitty, to see his once little girl pale and sleeping, her own little girl in the cot next to her. And the baby opened her eyes at his approach, and he gasped.

"Dad?" Kitty, still worried about her father, said. "Are you OK?"

"What? Oh, yes, I'm... look..." he moved aside for Kitty and Tom to get a better look of their niece. Kitty smiled widely and Tom took his phone from his pocket for a picture.

"She's looking at us!" he said, and then – entirely unused to babies as he is, "Is she?"

"Yes," Graham whispered. "Though we're probably just shapes to her. She can't focus properly yet." And as he spoke, the baby's face screwed up and then her bottom lip protruded slightly and without a moment's hesitation, she let out a wail. The three of them looked at each other and then at Annie, who was already stirring.

"Hello," she said, and it was unclear whether she was speaking to them or her baby. "You're here." Then she looked at her dad. "Can you pass her to me?"

"Really?"

"Yes, really! I can't pick her up myself. I think she might want feeding. I don't know. I'm just assuming that if she's crying she's hungry."

"It's a sensible conclusion to draw," Graham said, and stepped forward, reaching down to hold his granddaughter for the very first time. "Oh," he breathed in deeply as his hands met her tiny form, and thoughts of me whooshed through him as I tried to join him in this action, to feel what he was feeling. And he picked her up, solid and strong, like the grandad I know he is going to be, and held her warm, brand-newness to him for a couple of moments, soothing her, and for a moment she quietened and looked at him. But it didn't last long. And a midwife appeared, and helped Annie to sit up and hold the. baby to herself, and latch that tiny little mouth on to her nipple, and Tom tried not to look, while Kitty gazed in admiration and awe, feeling every inch the little sister as Annie took a step further ahead of her in life once more.

And when the baby was fed they took in in turns to hold her, and Alex returned, and they took photos and laughed together, filled with a joy which would have seemed impossible twelve months ago.

Alex is in as soon as he can be the following morning, having sat in his car eating an Egg McMuffin and slurping a coffee. When he'd finally left the previous evening, he'd gone round to Donna's and told her all about it and she'd been pleased for him, but worried too.

Alex was so full of the joys of fatherhood, and praise for Annie, and love for his baby. Had she been mad to think there would be room for her in his life?

But Alex had seen this. Although he had never really understood Annie, despite growing up with her, he easily got Donna. He could see she was slightly crestfallen and he put his arms around her. "It doesn't mean anything, you know. Well, it does," he clarified, "it means the world. I'm a dad. I have a daughter. But it doesn't change anything for us. Unless you want it to?" He was suddenly full of doubt himself. Perhaps Donna would not want to be lumbered with somebody who had a child from another relationship.

"Of course I don't!" she laughed, and put her hands either side of his face. "I'm so happy for you."

"I love you, Donna," Alex said without thinking, leaning forward to kiss her. Should he have said that? Was it the emotion of the day taking over? He raked through his feelings quickly, wondering if he should have held back but no, he thought, it was true. He laughed with wonder at how life could change, and how quickly. "I love you."

"I love you too," she had said, and kissed him back then led him upstairs.

Alex is thinking of this now as he chews the last mouthful of muffin and pulls the lid from his cup to enjoy the dregs of his coffee. It was a guilty pleasure and not one that Annie would have encouraged, but that had no bearing now. He was free to do as he pleased, and Donna was much more easy-going. She wouldn't bat an eyelid if he worked his way through five Big Macs in a row.

Getting out of the car and binning the evidence, he heads across the tarmac and through the early morning sunshine, passing people arriving at work and joining other new fathers waiting at the door. One has a little girl with him and Alex smiles at her, thinking of all that he has to look forward to. She clutches her dad's hand and smiles shyly at Alex.

And then they are allowed in, giving their names and their partner's, and hand-sanitising before moving onto the ward, which feels to Alex a bit like trespassing into an unknown and unknowable territory, with its all-female occupants and staff. Alex feels a sense of guilt on behalf of his gender and all that they have put these women through; how easy it is for them to glide into fatherhood, having put in the minimum of effort to get there. A few moments of pleasure for them and hopefully their partners, but then their part was done while these incredible women went through months of body changes, sickness, stretch marks, swollen ankles, changing tastes, hormones, exhaustion… high blood pressure in Annie's case… He is well aware of the imbalance in this situation and he keeps his head down as he walks along towards Annie's room, as if the other women might boo him and pelt him with rotten fruit and vegetables. They probably should, he thinks. He'd take it, as a representative of all the men. He'd take anything, to get to see his daughter again.

And he knocks on the door, his heart beating in his throat, and tears at the ready once more as he enters to find Annie sitting up eating breakfast, their daughter lying in her cot but wide awake.

"Hold her," Annie says, without even a greeting. Then she remembers herself. "Get as many cuddles in as you like."

She smiles at Alex but he feels like the gap between them has widened again; her experience has grown rapidly and it seems like she is already streets ahead, a pro at motherhood while he needs L plates.

"Hello," he says though, smilingly, to his daughter as he lifts her up, knowing there is no room for doubt when it comes to her. He has to step up and convince himself and her that he is worthy of being her dad.

"Olive?" Annie asks, and he looks at her then at her breakfast – toast and marmalade and a cup of tea – confused.

"I mean, shall we call her Olive?"

Alex feels a smile on his lips – a near-laugh – but

then he sees Annie is serious and he tries it out.

"Olive." He rolls the name around his mouth, surprised to find it feels right. "Yes. I would never have thought of it, but I like it. But I wondered – did you want to name her after your mum?"

"I don't know. It has crossed my mind," Annie admits. "But she's her own person, isn't she? And what about your mum?"

"She wouldn't mind," Alex says but they both know she would.

"How about Olive Celia Ruth?"

"Oh, Annie. Really? We could have Olive Ruth Celia?"

"No, no, I think we should have your mum's first." Annie deliberately doesn't mention a surname because she wants hers back, and she wants her daughter to have it too. But that is for another time.

And Alex sits next to Annie's bed, holding their little girl to his chest while Annie eats, comforting Olive when she begins to cry, insisting that Annie finish her breakfast first. They have so much to come, these three, and it won't all be easy, by any means. But right now they are encased in a bubble of newness, and wonder, tucked away from the rest of the world and what is often called real life. I feel privileged to be a witness but I know that I too need to leave them to it.

26

At the long barrow my friends gather around me, offering congratulations.

Teresa and Kiran, both fortunate enough to have lived to a similar age to me and who have grown-up children of their own; both desperate to be grandmothers but also desperately sad that they will never get to play that role in that world.

Charlotte, whose boys are growing up without her but, she hopes, a long way off making her a grandmother just yet.

David, Terry and June, all actively missed by their grandchildren.

Adam, and Jasmine, perhaps thinking that they never even got to be parents – though they are kind enough not to show it.

All of them, in fact, bring a glow of excitement and wonder, helping me focus on the happiness of the occasion.

"Annie has a daughter!" Kiran exclaims. "And what a wonderful role model of a mother she will be."

"And Kitty's going to be such a fantastic auntie,"

gushes Teresa, who has definitely developed a soft spot for my younger daughter.

"Olive is a lovely name too," says David. "My grandma was called Olive."

"And they've named her after you as well!" says Jasmine. "That must feel so special."

"It does. It's lovely."

"She'll think of you when she hears it," says Teresa. "And she may not be able to feel your presence the same way she could before she was born but you'll always be part of her life."

I know it's true. And I know there is nothing I can do about it anyway. But it's hard, seeing my family move on without me. I was about fifty, I think, and the children in their teens, when I began to feel my age, and to contemplate them moving on and moving out – and eventually, perhaps, making me a grandmother. My sister was still alive then and we'd laugh about getting older, but reflect on the better points of it – the not caring so much what people thought of us, and not feeling so much like we had to apologise for things.

I really remember that; how at first in our marriage if Graham and I had argued I'd be the one to apologise, whether or not I believed I was in the wrong, just to smooth things over and be at peace once more. As we aged, my sister had enough of her husband altogether, and asked for a divorce, whereas I still loved Graham, just in a different way. And it wasn't that I couldn't imagine life without him – I could, and often did – but

I knew that I would miss him. And despite his affair (this was before I met Nick so I was at this point squeaky clean in that respect) I knew that he loved me, and would look out for me. Above everything, Graham is a good man, and I knew that. But I was no longer desperate for his approval.

So getting older was not all bad, and occasionally – missing those days when the children were small – I would allow my imagination to run towards one day having grandchildren, and experiencing once more that feeling of little arms around my neck, lifting a still-sleepy child from their bed, them wrapping their legs around me and snuggling into my neck. I had envisaged myself as a supportive but non-intrusive grandparent, who would be there for my children and their partners without offering unwanted opinions – and also without being walked over. I had friends whose children were older than mine, who were already being called on for grandparent duties, spending weekends babysitting to enable their offsprings' social lives and missing out on their own. They would grumble about it yet allow it to continue. That, I decided, would not happen to me. What I had never imagined was that when the time came, I would already be gone from that world.

While I am not mean or self-centred enough not to realise that today is a day of celebration, I do also know I need some time to myself, to reflect. They see that, my friends, and they drift away, and I turn to the outdoors, where all is life. Out here, the autumn sun is beating down, warming the stones of the long barrow entrance and making the insects glow as they dart over the tops of the long grasses and the dying heads of the last wildflowers of the year.

The long-tailed tits are playing in the branches of the big oak tree, and I watch them for a while as the breeze blows the occasional leaf from its safehold, letting it fall, twirling, onto the surface of the pond below. My eyes turn to survey the landscape, knowing that the following weeks will see dramatic change here, the flaxen fields transformed to muted browns, shorn to a low wintering stubble. The occasional trees will change colour and, eventually, be laid entirely bare. Tom and Cecily will come in search of their owls, which first brought them together, and Mavis may or may not be with them. I think she would prefer to stay at home by the fire these days.

I can hear the road with its occasional heavy vehicles, tractors and lorries, rattling and bumping along, for the most part entirely unaware that over here, across the fields, this place sits humming with life. I like it that way.

I sit, alone, letting the sun pour its heat into me, filling me up, and offer thanks for the safe delivery of my granddaughter, and the happiness of my daughter, and her brother and sister and father. The joy that this child will bring to their world, they deserve.

I just have to let this all wash over me. Accept it and, more than that, appreciate it. Love it. My daughter is a mother! It is wonderful. And it really is – full of wonder. In the autumn light, I close my eyes and feel golden.

Later, much later, I am alerted by the sound of a car. And I know immediately who it belongs to.

Alex.

And I'm almost beside myself because I also know immediately what this means.

I move to watch the proceedings, knowing my long barrow friends are behind me – just far enough to give me some space but just near enough to see what's happening too.

He pulls up into the parking space, and he goes to the passenger side of the car, opening the door and graciously helping my daughter out of her seat. She moves slowly and painfully, straightening up so slowly, scared that she will hurt herself.

And Alex goes to the back door now, and he opens it and I hear him talking, in a voice I've never heard him use before, and it makes me smile. "Hello little one," he is saying. And he's nervous, I can feel it, the vibrations rippling their way across the long grasses, but he's trying to be strong and sure of himself, as he unfastens the straps that have been holding his tiny, perfect daughter in her seat, then lifts her to him. "You're so beautiful," he whispers, and he blushes when he sees Annie smiling at him.

I take a close look at my own beautiful daughter, seeing she is pale and tired but somehow more relaxed than I may ever have known her to be. *This is right,* she is thinking, again and again. *This is so right.*

"Can you manage? Walking, I mean?" Alex asks her anxiously.

"I think so. It's not far. And I'm supposed to be moving about, building myself back up again."

"We'll bring the pram," he says decisively. "Here, wait. If we bring her in the pram then you can use that for support if you need to, or I can help you and push the pram. I just don't want you to get halfway there and need some help, and for me to be holding Olive..."

Alex is babbling a little, anticipating an objection from Annie, slightly bewildered when none comes. And he kisses Olive on her head, laying her carefully back in her car seat, then he goes to the boot and gets out the pram, and Annie has to hold herself back from showing him how to put it up correctly, as she knows he has to do it himself, and she knows he will get there.

Who is this patient woman? I don't know how long it will last, but I like it.

And Alex does work it out, then he fastens Olive into her seat again, unclicks it and lifts the whole thing out, then slots it into place. And he pushes her next to Annie, who looks down on her daughter, then at her ex-husband, then she smiles and slides her arm through his.

Together they walk, taking their time, a family of three, towards the long barrow. And I wait until they reach me, and then I move with them and my friends here move back, forming a line either side of the path as we go to the entrance, and Annie takes her arm back, pushes the code into the lock, and opens the door. As she does so, she finds tears wetting her cheeks and a lump in her throat that she gulps back.

"Come and meet your grandma," she whispers softly to Olive, and she wishes that she were able to carry her in, to hold her tiny form against her as she enters the first chamber, but instead she walks ahead and it is Alex who unfastens their baby again, lifts and carries her into the womb of the barrow, where darkness and peace unite. Annie sits on the stone seat, next to my niche. Alex places the little blanketed bundle into her arms and I surround my daughter and granddaughter, and they feel it, the warmth, soaked up from the sun and sustained by the intense, immense and infinite love I have for them both.

Alex watches the light dance across them, filtering in from the outside, and he breathes deeply, moved by feelings of such tenderness and a desire to protect – *but not own*, he tells himself, still unable to extricate himself from anticipated criticism from Annie – these two people in front of him. *My child and her mother*. He sighs.

As for me, I maintain my form, wrapping my child and hers in love, willing them to know me, my feelings just as tender and protective as Alex's.

They don't light any candles or open the niche, and they don't stay long, but none of that matters. I know that no matter the pain or discomfort, or the fact that Annie doesn't really know that she believes I am here, she had to find the closest thing to introducing her baby to me, and this is just one of the ways that the love remains even though I have gone.

Back at their house – Annie's house, or Annie's and Olive's, to be precise, Alex settles them both in the lounge and then goes into the kitchen.

It is at once strange and so natural at the same time. He no longer lives here, he is well aware of that fact, but it still feels like home. And he puts on the kettle, to make some tea, then he hears Olive crying, and Annie calls him, and he lifts their daughter to Annie so that she can feed, and Annie looks at him with tears in her eyes.

"I can't do any of this myself," she wails, shocking herself with an onslaught of emotion brought on by hormones, post-op and emotional exhaustion.

"You will," Alex soothes, sliding down onto the gap on the seat next to her. "You just need to heal, and get your strength back. Would you – would you like me to stay here tonight?"

Annie looks at him through her red-rimmed eyes and he immediately fears he's said the wrong thing.

But – "Yes please," she says. "But then what?"

"Then what?"

"I mean – I'll still be like this tomorrow. Useless," she clarifies.

"Annie," says Alex, watching their daughter feed and hoping very much that Annie doesn't mind, "I will stay with you as long as you want. Or I'm sure Kitty, or Tom, or your dad…"

"I'd like you to. If you don't mind?" she sniffles.

"Of course I don't!" says Alex and for maybe the first time in his life, Annie has made him feel like she needs him. "I'll stay here as long as you like."

Later, after Annie has had a sleep and Alex has watched a film with his daughter safely in his arms, he makes them some pasta and salad for dinner, and they sit at the table to eat, and it's almost like the old days, except it's not.

Alex's phone pings and he checks it, knowing he does not have to answer to Annie anymore.

"Donna?" she asks.

"Yeah." He types out a quick message to her. She is keen to see Olive, he knows, but she doesn't want to push it, and neither does he, but he is very intent on making sure there's no perceived threat from Annie. Nothing more to his staying with her than looking after her while she's recovering, and getting to know his baby.

I understand, Donna said. **Honestly, I totally get it.**

And she does, but that doesn't mean it's easy. Still, if she wants this to work, she tells herself, then she needs to be grown up and sensible and keep her emotions in check.

Thank you, Alex sent back. **You're amazing. I love you xxxx**

That made her feel a little bit better.

And Annie, though not a fan of phones at the table, is enjoying all the messages of congratulations she's receiving, and she's also waiting to hear from somebody in particular. And:

Oh my god! The message almost bursts through the phone as though it's imbued with his energy. **I can't believe it! I lost my fucking phone in a taxi and I've only just got it back and – I can't believe you've had your baby. And a C-Section, you must have been scared. You must be sore. Can you send me a picture? Of Olive, I mean, not your poor belly.**

She smiles, which does not escape Alex's attention, and then she sends a photo, receiving another message packed with energy and exclamations in return. Then a follow-up which reads:

I haven't stopped thinking about you. And worrying how I'd find you if I didn't get my phone back. I

mean, I would have found you. That sounds scary! I mean, I'd have worked out how to get in touch somehow. I couldn't let this slide. X

And so Annie and Alex sit at the table, eating, checking their phones, and occasionally talking, then at the sound of Olive crying in the next room they both rise and go through to her, leaving their plates and glasses on the table, to be tidied up later. Like I said, it's almost like the old days, except it's not.

27

Fast-forward to the day they've been dreading. The anniversary of the day I died. I feel self-conscious and self-important calling it that. It's a year since that day though, when I finally sank under and let the illness swallow what was left of me.

Graham awakes sluggishly, Mavis sound asleep next to him, her poor tired body reminding him of me, and immediately he remembers what day it is. "Oh Ruth," he sobs and sinks back against the pillow, allowing the grief in, making space for it. Mavis snores on.

Kitty, in her childhood bedroom, has been awake for some time and she hears her dad, and his exclamation, and subsequent anguish. She squirms a little at having such access, and takes herself downstairs, glumly filling the kettle and remembering how many times I would have stood at the sink, the very same kettle in my hand, performing exactly the same act. She forces herself to think this, like she is punishing herself. But for what?

And Tom, also in his childhood room – which is currently also his adulthood room – lies wide awake, his arm aching around Cecily's shoulder. He wants to move it but he doesn't. She fits so nicely into that curve of his armpit, and he has no wish to disturb her or to kickstart the reality of this day.

Over at Annie's, she is waking to a quiet house. Alex is not there, she having given him his marching orders – but in a surprisingly considerate way, for Annie – a couple of days before.

"Wouldn't you want me to be here for Ruth's anniversary?" he'd asked.

"No, really, I need to get on now. With life. And so do you."

Even Annie had been sensitive to the fact that this would not be easy on Alex. She had kicked him out once before and now she was doing the same again, but in very different circumstances. Because Alex has been fantastic. A rock. On the rare occasions she would creep onto Facebook and observe other people's posts, silently (never Liking or Commenting), Annie would occasionally see an old school friend or workmate wishing their partner a happy birthday or happy anniversary, proclaiming them to be their rock, and she had quietly scorned this expression, thinking it was weak. Now though, and perhaps it was easier because Alex was no longer her partner, she found that she really could appreciate his role in her life since she'd come back from hospital. Uncomplainingly and unflinchingly, he had been up and down, lifting, carrying, changing nappies, putting Olive down to sleep, picking her up again when she needed feeding. Cooking, washing nappies, and washing Annie's clothes too. But his paternity leave was at an end and it seemed like a good time for Annie to begin practising her independence.

"But you know you can come round whenever. I mean, call first…" That seemed quite harsh. But it was necessary, Annie told herself, and she'd seen a flash of resentment cross his face. "But Alex, it's just – it's got to be that way, OK? But I'm not ever going to be trying to keep you away from Olive, and Donna is welcome too, and when I'm not breastfeeding anymore –" already Annie was half eager to stop, finding the itching and the urgent filling of her breasts quite hard to countenance, yet at the same time not ready to give up that absolutely unique bond between her and her baby – "it will get easier, OK? You'll be able to take her out. Have her overnight…" That also seemed hard to imagine, but just as Alex had to accept his limitations, Annie knew she would have to cede some control to him.

And it would give her a chance to work, she thought, glad to find that she did still want to. But not yet. Not just yet.

There is no surprise for Annie when she wakes; no sudden remembering or realisation. Olive has already had her up three times since midnight and Annie is more than aware what day it is.

She hears her phone ping. It's the family WhatsApp. Kitty has sent a photo of the five of us, and one of me.

Love you all, she has added.

Annie wells up. She looks at her daughter sleeping soundly now, in the Moses basket at the end of the bed, and she sits herself up quietly, hoping for a few moments of peace, and solitude. She is less sore now but still reluctant to make any sudden movements. But she takes herself off for a shower and is at first gratified, and then panicked, when she turns the water off and the house is still quiet. She dashes as quickly as she can manage back to the bedroom and sees the reassuring rise and fall of her daughter's chest. Clearly her little girl has tired herself out with her night-time exploits.

"It's alright for you," Annie murmurs, then she picks up her phone and replies to Kitty:

Love you too. All of you. And she sends a photo of sleeping Olive. **She does too.**

The plan had been for Graham to pick up Annie and Olive and bring them over to our house, then for all of them to come to the long barrow, before returning home for lunch. As it turns out, it is tipping it down, in stark contrast to this day a year before when the sun shone on, blithely ignoring the fact that I was gone. Gleaming in the face of so much grief.

Graham drives determinedly across town to Annie's house, the windscreen wipers valiantly rushing this way and that, squeaking as they clear away the downpour only to be thwarted afresh. It's fitting, he thinks, this weather. It matches his mood. But when he sees Olive, he can't help but smile. "You're a little ray of sunshine, aren't you?" he sings to her, cradling her and marvelling at how she has already grown.

And he whisks them back home, where Tom has lit a fire, and Mavis has taken up her place in front of it, the heat soothing her aches and pains.

Kitty, meanwhile, is putting the finishing touches to a little buffet: bread is warming in the oven, and there's a substantial range of cheeses on the table, with pickled onions and chutneys, roasted garlic and cherry tomatoes; houmous; crackers, breadsticks, coleslaw... way too much really but I am touched. This is the kind of lunch I used to like on days like this; low-key but plentiful and relaxed, people helping themselves. On a day like Boxing Day, when we might have wider family visiting, I'd put it all out and let people take a plate and seat themselves wherever they liked. It took the pressure off me, to be honest, after all the build-up to Christmas.

Kitty hums to herself then she stops, remembering that's just what I used to do. And she hears Graham opening the front door, greeting Alex, who has arrived with Celia and James. Kitty goes through to say hello but she hangs back, still feeling a bit awkward around Alex. She watches Graham shaking James' hand, and Annie handing Olive to Celia, bypassing Alex, who really doesn't mind. He is just glad to be included. He'd half-wanted to ask if Donna could come but no, he knew it was too soon for that – and too personal an occasion for my family too. She has been to see Annie and the baby though, and it wasn't too painful, all things considered.

Even Cecily has stepped back from this particular event, and she has in fact come to the barrow, where she finds Derek and Val sheltering from the rain, and that Scottish man who sometimes comes for a walk up here, sitting on the bench outside, under an umbrella. "Do you want to come in? Till the worst of it's passed?" she asks kindly.

"Oh no pet, but thank you," Nick smiles, thinking that maybe the worst of it will never pass. But he also thinks of Claire, and their tentative plans to meet sometime, in Birmingham, for a meal and a show, and he wonders if he can perhaps see a little patch of blue sky after all.

Back in the heart of our home, where we brought back all three of our babies from the hospital, and watched them grow up, I sit by the fire with Mavis, listening to her gently snoring, and watching the room fill up, first with Alex and his parents, and Olive, then Annie, Tom,

Graham, and finally Kitty, still feeling a bit shy, and maybe the one most affected by the significance of the day. They sit leaning forward, perched on the edge of their seats, balancing plates on their knees. Celia is not really keen on this kind of eating, preferring to sit at a table, but she is keen to fit in and keep everyone on side. She's looking forward to a cuddle with her granddaughter in due course, and Alex has promised to talk to Annie again about Celia babysitting from time to time. Annie is already expecting this and quite prepared to say yes. Now that Olive is here and she's realised how time-consuming and self-consuming a baby is, she sees that there will be no harm in sharing out her care a little – and since Celia's role in Olive's birth she has thawed towards her anyway.

Graham exclaims, leaving his plate on a nearby table, and returning with a tray bearing a bottle of champagne, and seven glasses. "I thought we should have a little toast to Ruth," he says, and the room goes quiet but Celia smiles and says that's a wonderful idea, and what a lovely woman I was. James agrees with her, and Annie smiles a slightly tight-lipped smile.

Tom, genial as always, hands round the glasses while Graham struggles with the cork and then nearly breaks the light fitting as it flies out with a huge pop, so loud it even disturbs Mavis, though only briefly.

Graham pours everyone a glass, watching carefully to make sure not a drop is spilled as the liquid froths and bubbles up near the rim. Then when everyone has a drink he stands, near the fireplace – next to me – and clears his throat.

"Well this time last year I would never have pictured myself standing here with a glass of champagne, of all things. But it's been an eventful year and despite everything we have things to be grateful for. Our beautiful Olive, for starters. And though I miss Ruth–" he pauses here, choked, but coughs again and recovers himself – "maybe every minute of every day, she was somebody who always saw the good, in people, and in life. And I know she would be happy to see us together like this. And to know that she is remembered, always. To Ruth."

Annie is staring at her glass while he speaks, while Kitty is letting the tears roll freely down her cheeks. Tom swallows hard and looks at the photo of me that sits on the tiny table near the fireplace. Celia and James are respectfully quiet, while Alex's eyes are shining too. Kitty happens to glance across and see this.

"To Ruth," they say in response, or, "To Mum."

And I feel flattered, and honoured, and warmed through. And then Olive cries, which is perfect really, as nobody is quite sure how to move on from that moment, and Celia moves to pick her up, then looks at Annie, to check that's OK, and Annie nods and smiles.

James pats the seat next to him and engages Graham in a discussion about the steam train due to travel through the town station next week, and Tom starts talking to Annie about her work, while Celia gazes dreamily down at her granddaughter.

For the first time in a long time, Alex and Kitty find themselves thrown together.

Kitty looks at Alex.

"So…" she says.

"So what?" he says, and he smiles, and Kitty can't help smiling back. As he turns automatically to check on his daughter, she takes the chance to look at Alex, properly, and finds her feelings towards him restored to how they always used to be. And now, she finds, admiration is added to the mix. For she's seen the way he's stepped in, and the way he cares, not just for Olive but for Annie too, despite everything. And he cared about me too, and she can only love him for that.

I blow lightly on the flames of the fire, making them flicker a little, but nobody notices, and I think that is really how it should be. The room is full of talk and laughter, and love, and though the cold rain clatters down on the roof and the wind rails against the windows, try as they might they are not getting in.

Acknowledgements

I am as always so grateful to everybody who has helped me get a book to completion, and I will start as I often do with my beta readers (and hope very much I don't forget anyone in the following list). These wonderful people read early versions of books for me, entirely free of charge, and offer their feedback and support. I am so appreciative of this, and of them. It's lovely to think there are people out there who I have never met who are happy to do this. So the biggest thanks to (in no particular order): Marilynn Wrigley, Tracey Shaw, Rebecca Leech, Sandra Francis, Jean Crowe, Alison Lassey, Ginnie Ebbrell, Amanda Tudor, Roz Osborn, Mandy Chowney-Andrews, Hilary Kerr, Julie Moxham and Denise Armstrong. Having said I have never met any of them, that is not quite true – I do know Denise and I know she has also been to Soulton Long Barrow and seen that magical place for herself.

I would also like to take this opportunity to wish Marilynn Wrigley and her soon-to-be husband (in fact by the time this book is published there will be no need for 'soon-to-be!) huge congratulations. It is a pleasure to have got to know you Marilynn, by email and through your own writing, and I wish you and Robert all the happiness you deserve. I would like to say more but this is your story and not mine to share but I absolutely love it.

Big thanks to Josie Sandhu, my not-quite-niece but daughter of my cousin Ruth, who is just as great as the Ruth in these books and has been a steady and lovely presence throughout my mum's illness and beyond. These days our wild swims are some of my very favourite times. I know how much my mum loved Ruth and her sister Martha, their mum Joyce and perhaps most of all their dad Gez, my mum's big brother. But this is for Josie, who has kindly stepped in to proofread for me and offered some brilliant advice on my books and my website, and who is just as clever, and amazing, as her mum. (Probably more so but don't tell Ruth I said that.)

Of course no book would be complete without an enormous THANK YOU to Catherine Clarke, whose amazing talents bring all of my books to life. I feel like each time she sends me a cover I think it's my favourite! But I do love this one, with the light falling across Ruth's face. Thank you Catherine, for the covers and of course, most importantly, for your friendship.

I also owe thanks to Katie Jenkin; a friend I made during antenatal classes in 2009, and somebody whose friendship has weathered all the various life events we've both been through in the intervening years. Katie was a huge support while my mum was ill and I've never forgotten that. She was also able to help me out a bit with this book in sharing some of her professional medical knowledge – but any mistakes or errors are all mine. I was just very grateful to be able to bounce some ideas off her and get her advice.

This book is dedicated to my very good friend Leanne, and her mum Trish, who died this October. Leanne's dad Pete died three years ago and he and Trish were lovely; always welcoming to my family when we came to visit and, like Leanne, warm and generous and kind. I have known Leanne a long time and had been planning to dedicate a book to her as not only a brilliant ex-work colleague, ex-housemate, and fan of Most Haunted, but as a truly incredible, strong woman who takes what life throws at her and shoulders it all. Without, as far as I can tell, complaining. Most importantly of all, she laughs at my jokes. Love you, Le-le.

The name for Alex and Annie's baby comes from my good friend Gill's mum – Olive. I never knew Olive but Gill has a special place in my life, as somebody I have come to know thanks to my books and who has been so kind and generous to me and my family. Thank you Gill x

As always I can thank my family, Chris, Laura, Edward and not forgetting Ash and Willow, our very much loved dogs who bring so much into our lives, and don't ask for much except for constant attention, never-ending affection, ball and frisbee throwing and an endless supply of food and treats. I have always loved dogs in books and in real life (despite having been scared of them as a child) and these two have had a huge impact on our family while we've been dealing with loss and grief just as the Hebdens have (though thankfully with less drama). Mavis is a little nod to them and the important place pets have in our lives. Thank you of course to my dad Ted Rogers, for his endless support and for once again reviewing my work in progress.

And thank you, as always, to my mum, Rosemary. It's obvious that her death has been the driving force behind this series and I miss her very much. But I remember her kindness and the way she had time for so many people, and I try to follow her example, and also try to convey the love she filled our lives with through my books. As Ruth says (and I have my friend Fran to thank for these words, or this sentiment at least), the love remains. And long may it last.

What Comes Next

An introduction to the Hebden family as they celebrate their first Christmas without much loved wife and mother, Ruth. Set entirely on Christmas Day, at the long barrow where Ruth's ashes have been placed. It is Ruth herself who tells the story, seeing and hearing all.

This short, festive story is an exploration of another side of this time of year normally packed with family, friends and festivities. It is nevertheless uplifting and engaging, and full of Christmas spirit.

The first full-length novel begins with an illicit kiss, with Ruth its only witness but unable to say or do anything about it. As her family begin to find their way through their grief and navigate new situations and changing relationships, Ruth herself has much to learn as she comes to terms with her new situation and the fact that she can now only watch as life moves on without her.

Coming Back to Cornwall

A bestselling series that refuses to end!

The whole Coming Back to Cornwall series is being made into audiobooks so you that you can listen to the adventures of Alice, Julie and Sam while you drive, cook, clean, go to sleep... whatever, wherever! Books One to Five are available now.

Connections
Books One to Four

Each story focuses on a different character all inextricably linked within the small Cornish town they call home.

Individual novels

Writing the Town Read: Katharine's first novel. "I seriously couldn't put it down and would recommend it to anyone who doesn't like chick lit, but wants a great story."

Looking Past - a story of motherhood and growing up without a mother.

"Despite the tough topic the book is full of love, friendships and humour. Katharine Smith cleverly balances emotional storylines with strong characters and witty dialogue, making this a surprisingly happy book to read."

Amongst Friends - a back-to-front tale of friendship and family, set in Bristol.

"An interesting, well written book, set in Bristol which is lovingly described, and with excellent characterisation. Very enjoyable."

Printed in Dunstable, United Kingdom